About the Author

As a child who grew up without parental support, I developed a deep passion for mental health advocacy. Through volunteer work at childcare homes for victims of domestic violence and sexual abuse, I've made a meaningful impact. Providing a support system for these children is an honor I cherish, and it's gratifying to know that my efforts have positively influenced their lives.

By contributing funds for their basic needs, such as toiletries, clothes, food, stationery, and education, I've helped create a better world for those who need it most. I've discovered a meaningful way to give back to the universe what I received as a child.

Later, as I navigated my struggles and sought inner peace, I uncovered the powerful truth that self-love and accessing bliss within are the keys to unlocking solutions to any problem. I came to the profound realization that loving myself and cultivating happiness within my being is the key to overcoming any obstacle. Through this self-love and inner contentment, I have been able to tap into my strength and resilience and ultimately find solutions to even the most daunting setbacks.

With over two decades of life experience, I have amassed a wealth of invaluable experience and techniques for self-improvement and healing that can immensely benefit those in need. Now that I have progressed as a certified life coach, I am excited to announce the release of my new book, *Bliss Access Within You*. This book is a reader for anyone seeking happiness and inner peace.

Dr. Shanthi Ramaiah

BLISS ACCESS WITHIN YOU

AUSTIN MACAULEY PUBLISHERS®
LONDON • CAMBRIDGE • NEW YORK • SHARJAH

ISBN – 9789948731054 – (Paperback)
ISBN – 9789948731078 – (E-Book)

Application Number: MC-10-01-4970573
Age Classification: E

The age group that matches the content of the books has been classified according to the age classification system issued by the UAE Media Council.

First Published 2024
AUSTIN MACAULEY PUBLISHERS FZE
Sharjah Publishing City
P.O Box [519201]
Sharjah, UAE
www.austinmacauley.ae
+971 655 95 202

Acknowledgements

I am writing to express my sincere gratitude for the multitude of valuable life experiences that I have been blessed with. These experiences have helped shape me into who I am today and contributed immensely to my personal growth and development. I am also profoundly grateful for the many extraordinary individuals who have crossed my path and have made a lasting impact on my life. Their guidance, support, and wisdom have been invaluable to me and have helped me overcome many obstacles and challenges along the way.

As I reflect on my journey, I am particularly grateful to those who have played a critical role in the successful completion of this book. Their unwavering commitment, dedication, and hard work have been instrumental in bringing this project to fruition. I cannot express enough how much their contributions have meant to me, and I feel truly blessed to have had the opportunity to work with such talented and inspiring individuals.

Although I must keep my acknowledgement brief and concise, I want to ensure that everyone who has contributed to my journey knows how much I appreciate them. Thank you from the bottom of my heart for all you have done for me.

I express my deep gratitude toward all the individuals who have participated in my keynote speeches and training sessions and those who have availed of my services as clients in the past few years. I am thoroughly impressed by your unwavering devotion to blissfulness and other impactful strategies. Your steadfast commitment to these methodologies will bring immense progress in your professional endeavors, business pursuits, and personal growth. Please maintain your exceptional work ethic and unrelenting focus on self-improvement with blissfulness.

I am truly grateful for your unwavering support and encouragement, which helped me complete this book ahead of schedule. Your consistent assistance kept me motivated and focused throughout the writing process. I cannot thank you enough for your valuable contribution to this achievement.

I want to extend my most profound appreciation to my beloved family for their unyielding support. This literary masterpiece I created would not have been possible without their unwavering dedication and encouragement. Their admirable compassion and thoughtfulness toward others are my constant inspiration and drive, making me want to push forward every day.

Dear Dr. Kamal Mishra, I am grateful for your invaluable contribution to my book project. I truly appreciate your enthusiasm and precision, despite your busy academic schedule and tight deadlines. Thanks to your help, the book turned out significantly better than it would have if I had written it alone. Your contribution has been instrumental in launching my writing career.

Table of Contents

Chapter 1: Bliss

During a recent conversation, I brought up the title of a book that delves into the relationship between happiness and physical and mental well-being. Naturally, my peers were intrigued and inquired further about the topic.

Reflecting on my significant life-threatening health journey, I recalled being diagnosed with mixed connective tissue autoimmune disease in 2007. At the time, the side effects of the prescribed medication were more burdensome than the disease itself. Looking back, I now recognize that stress and mental strain significantly exacerbated my illness. This realization underscores that our overall well-being, including our mental health, profoundly impacts our psychological and physical health.

There is a growing body of evidence that suggests that mental stress and our general state of well-being can have a detrimental effect on our overall health.

After thorough consideration, it is crucial to realize that achieving a state of bliss, composure, and tranquility within oneself is essential in preventing and alleviating severe physical and psychological ailments. The origin of this book's title, "Bliss Access within you", can be traced back to a specific and unique source, one of my life journeys, which is the inspiration for its name. Without further delay, let's explore the bliss.

What is bliss?

Bliss refers to a state of being extremely happy and content. It is a feeling of complete satisfaction and fulfillment. People usually describe this state as "in the zone" where everything seems perfect, and nothing could go wrong. The sources of this state of bliss could differ for different people. Some people find it in nature, while others find it in relationships or creative activities. However, bliss is a rare and valuable emotion.

Experiencing moments of bliss can have a tremendous impact on our overall well-being. It activates the release of naturally occurring chemicals in our brains, such as dopamine and serotonin, which positively affect our bodies and minds. These effects include reducing stress levels, increasing pain tolerance, and boosting our immune system. It's incredible to think that such simple moments of joy can have such powerful benefits.

The experience of bliss can offer many spiritual benefits for individuals seeking to connect with their inner selves and the world around them. One of the most notable advantages is a heightened sense of connection to others, fostering deeper relationships, and a greater understanding of empathy.

Additionally, the experience of bliss can promote a feeling of oneness with the universe, allowing individuals to tap into a greater sense of purpose and meaning in their lives. By embracing this powerful emotion, individuals may unlock new personal growth and spiritual fulfillment.

Take a few simple steps to cultivate more joy and happiness in life. Begin by recognizing the things that bring you the most delight. Then, prioritize those activities in your daily routine. Finally, consider incorporating relaxation practices such as meditation-yoga Yoga. These techniques can help to soothe your mind and body, allowing you to embrace the experience of blissfully.

Bliss is a state of being that is both fleeting and elusive. However, by following these tips, you can increase your chances of experiencing it more often. And when you do, you will know you truly live in the moment.

Here are some additional things to consider about bliss:

- There is no denying that even the briefest moment of experiencing pure bliss can profoundly impact our lives, despite its fleeting nature. Whether it's the feeling of warm sunshine on our skin, the sound of laughter shared with loved ones, or the taste of our favorite food, these moments of pure joy can bring us a sense of happiness that stays with us long after they've passed. It is a reminder that despite life's challenges, there is always something to be grateful for and a reason to keep pushing forward.
- Reaching a state of complete happiness and contentment, or bliss can be challenging. This is because it requires us to let go of our emotional ties to specific things, such as our expectations, fears, and ego. Only by freeing ourselves from these attachments can we experience true bliss and inner peace.

- While happiness is undoubtedly a significant component of the experience of bliss, it is not the only factor at play. True pleasure can encompass a range of emotions, such as a pervasive feeling of peace, a deep sense of contentment, or the overwhelming sensation of being loved. These elements combine to create a truly profound and transformative state of being.

The concept of bliss is a highly personal and subjective experience unique to everyone. While there is no definitive way to encounter this state of being, it may be closer than one initially perceives if one remains open and receptive to the possibility.

What are the benefits of accessing bliss?

Allow me to introduce you to the many benefits of experiencing a state of bliss. It provides a sense of deep contentment and happiness and can positively impact your physical and mental health. Studies have shown that regularly accessing feelings of bliss can lower stress levels, improve heart health, and boost overall well-being. So why explore the advantages of this beautiful state and see how it can enhance your life?

Reduced stress:

Bliss can release chemicals, such as dopamine and serotonin, in the brain, which can profoundly reduce stress. These chemicals are known to have a calming effect on the body and mind, resulting in decreased anxiety levels and an overall stress reduction. With the ability to release such chemicals, bliss can be a valuable tool for those looking to manage their stress levels and maintain a healthy mental state.

Increased pain tolerance:

According to recent studies, the experience of bliss has been shown to have a significant impact on our pain tolerance levels. This is because when we experience feelings of bliss, our brain releases various feel-good chemicals that help block pain signals from reaching our brain. As a result, we can better manage and tolerate pain, positively impacting our overall well-being.

Boosted immune system:

The sensation of bliss has been observed to have a notable impact on the immune system, as it triggers the release of chemicals that promote feelings of well-being. These chemicals have been found to stimulate the production of white blood cells, which are responsible for defending the body against various infections, diseases, and other harmful agents.

Consequently, experiencing bliss can be considered an effective way to boost immune system function and enhance overall health and well-being.

Improved sleep:

Feeling a sense of pure happiness or bliss can benefit your sleep quality. When you experience this state, your body releases chemicals that promote relaxation and calmness, making it easier to fall asleep and stay asleep throughout the night. The result is a more restful and rejuvenating sleep experience that can leave you feeling refreshed and energized when you wake up in the morning.

Increased creativity:

The state of experiencing bliss is known to impact creativity positively. This is because it enables the mind to become more receptive and open, which in turn allows for the generation of fresh ideas and insights to occur more effortlessly. By embracing a mindset of bliss, one can tap into a wellspring of creative potential that may have previously been untapped.

This can be particularly helpful when new and innovative solutions are required, as it enables individuals to approach problems from a unique perspective and find more effective ways to address them. Cultivating bliss can be a powerful tool for enhancing creativity and achieving tremendous success in various endeavors.

Deeper connection with others:

Experiencing bliss can profoundly impact our relationships, fostering a greater sense of openness and receptiveness toward others. The tranquil and contented state accompanying bliss can help cultivate deeper connections with those around us, ultimately enriching the quality of our social interactions and relationships.

A sense of oneness with the universe:

The state of experiencing bliss can be a profoundly transformative experience. Not only does it impart a sense of inner peace and tranquility, but it can also foster a powerful connection to the larger universe that surrounds us. Through this heightened awareness, we become more attuned to the rhythms and patterns of the natural world and can tap into a more profound sense of mindfulness that allows us to connect with something greater than ourselves.

Whether we achieve this state through meditation, yoga, or other spiritual practices, the benefits of experiencing bliss are undeniable. They can profoundly impact our overall well-being and sense of purpose in life.

Indulging in moments of bliss can profoundly impact our overall well-being, encompassing physical, mental, and emotional health. The benefits of experiencing such moments can be diverse depending on individual circumstances.

Identifying activities that bring you joy and happiness and carve out time for them is essential. Additionally, relaxation techniques such as meditation and yoga can help create a tranquil state of mind and body, making you more receptive to experiencing bliss. While the attainment of bliss may seem elusive, following these simple yet effective tips can significantly increase the likelihood of experiencing it more frequently.

By cherishing and savoring these moments of bliss, you can cultivate a sense of gratitude and live fully in the present moment.

How can you access bliss within?

Attaining a state of complete happiness can be challenging, and it requires conscious effort, dedication, and commitment. However, several methods can be helpful. It's important to remember that this state is achieved through internal work. Let me introduce some of these methods. To attain genuine happiness, it is crucial to strike a harmonious equilibrium among diverse techniques and integrate them into your day-to-day regimen.

By doing so, you can cultivate a sustainable approach that promotes happiness and overall well-being within yourself.

Meditate:

Meditation is a powerful tool for achieving inner peace and tranquility and can significantly enhance your overall well-being. With so many different meditation techniques to choose from, it's essential to take the time to explore your options and find the one that resonates most with you. Whether you prefer guided meditations, silent sitting, or something in between, committing to a regular meditation practice can help you cultivate greater mindfulness and emotional stability in your daily life.

So why not try it today and see how transformative this ancient practice can be?

Yoga:

Practicing yoga is an incredibly beneficial way to foster a deep connection between your body and mind. Physical poses, or asanas, effectively release tension and stress that can accumulate in the body over time. Additionally, the breathing exercises, or pranayama, incorporated into a yoga practice are particularly valuable for quieting the mind and promoting a sense of inner calm. Overall, practicing Yoga regularly can provide a multitude of benefits for both your physical and mental well-being.

Spend time in nature:

Immersing yourself in nature has been proven to impact mental health and overall well-being positively. Whether it's a leisurely walk through a local park, a challenging hike in the woods, or simply sitting outside and basking in the sunshine, spending time outdoors can help you feel more present and at peace. Nature's sights, sounds, and smells can awaken your senses and provide a sense of connection to the world around you.

So next time you feel stressed or overwhelmed, consider taking a break and spending time in nature. Your mind and body will thank you.

Listen to music:

Attaining a state of relaxation and inner peace can be a transformative experience that can be achieved effortlessly through the power of music. By carefully selecting music that has a calming and soothing effect on your mind and body, you can be fully immersed in its tranquil embrace, feeling the tension in your muscles slowly dissipate and your worries fade.

Whether it's the gentle melody of a classical piece, the rhythmic beats of a tranquil instrumental track, or the soft, soothing vocals of a ballad, the right kind of music can transport you to a place of pure bliss and tranquility, helping you to unwind from the stresses of daily life and find true inner peace.

Practice gratitude:

Practicing gratitude is a powerful practice that can help us focus on the good things in life and bring a sense of contentment. Taking a few moments each day to reflect on the things we are thankful for can profoundly impact our overall well-being. It is an excellent way to shift our perspective toward positivity and appreciate the small blessings we might have overlooked otherwise. So, let us take a step back and revel in the joy that gratitude can bring to our lives.

Practice forgiveness:

Releasing any grudges or resentments weighing you down is crucial to achieving genuine happiness. Though forgiving someone may be challenging, taking a moment to see things from their point of view can be helpful. Additionally, shifting your focus toward the positive aspects of your relationship can be beneficial rather than dwelling on any negative experiences. Doing so makes it easier to let go of releasing negative emotions and move toward a brighter future.

Do something you love:

Participating in activities that you find pleasurable and fulfilling can significantly increase your overall sense of happiness and contentment and eventually lead to pure joy. Whether indulging in a good book, jotting down your thoughts on paper, creating a masterpiece on canvas, practicing mindfulness, visualizations, affirmations, or grooving to your favorite tunes, it's essential to carve out time for these activities in your daily routine.

By prioritizing your happiness and engaging in activities that bring you joy, you can improve your well-being and lead a more fulfilling life.

Discovering what brings you a state of bliss can be a transformative experience. Finding a suitable activity is critical, whether it's the calming effects of meditation, the endorphin rush of exercise, or the soothing power of music. Taking the time to prioritize and engage in these activities can profoundly impact your well-being. You'll be amazed at how much more energized and content you feel by consistently incorporating these practices into your routine.

Consider experimenting with different techniques and approaches to optimize your results until you find what works best. Remember, achieving a state of bliss is all about finding the perfect balance between mind, body, and soul.

Be present at the moment:

Experiencing a state of bliss requires undivided attention toward the present moment. It entails relinquishing all thoughts and apprehensions about the past or future and directing complete concentration toward the present. By being fully present in the moment, one can genuinely relish and appreciate it to the fullest.

Let go of expectations:

Attaining genuine contentment is a complex process that necessitates relinquishing any preconceived notions one might have about what happiness should entail. One should strive to accept and embrace all feelings that surface, free from criticism or negative judgment. This approach can help pave the way for genuine happiness and inner peace within you.

Be open to new experiences:

Openness toward new experiences is essential as happiness can arise from unexpected sources. Trying out new things without hesitation is a great way to discover joy and contentment in life. Remember, bliss is a state of being unique to each individual and derived from within. There are many correct ways to experience it, but if you remain open to the possibility, you will discover that bliss comes from within.

Don't be afraid to ask for help:

If you're struggling to find happiness within yourself, consider contacting a qualified therapist, counselor, or mental health professional for assistance. These experts can work with you to identify any underlying issues preventing you from experiencing pure joy and provide practical techniques and strategies to help you achieve a more blissful state.

Whether you're dealing with past trauma, anxiety, depression, or other challenges, seeking the help of a professional can be a crucial step in your journey toward lasting happiness and fulfillment, and explore more ways to access bliss within yourself.

Chapter 2: Meditation

After experiencing a state of bliss, through my experience, I have realized that meditation regularly can be incredibly beneficial in enabling one to access a state of inner peace and tranquility commonly referred to as "Bliss". This state is characterized by a profound sense of calmness and a heightened awareness of one's surroundings, which can lead to a greater understanding of overall well-being and contentment from within.

By quieting the mind and focusing on the present moment, meditation can help to alleviate stress, reduce anxiety, and improve mental clarity and concentration. Making this practice a regular daily routine can provide numerous physical and psychological health benefits. Therefore, it's worth considering incorporating it into your daily routine. Without further delay, let's explore meditation.

What is meditation?

Meditation is a valuable tool in improving the health of the mind and body. One can effectively train the mind to become more aware and present by focusing on the present moment. This practice has been utilized for centuries by cultures worldwide, and various meditation methods are available. Among the most popular types are mindfulness, concentration, and visualization.

Each type of meditation offers unique benefits to the practitioner and it is essential to find the one that works best for each individual's needs. Regardless of the specific method chosen, the ultimate goal of meditation is to cultivate a state of inner peace and clarity that can lead to a more fulfilling life. There are different types of meditation:

Mindfulness meditation:

Mindfulness meditation is a technique that encourages you to concentrate on the present moment without any form of judgment. During this type of meditation, you can focus your attention on your breath, body, or thoughts. You can learn to manage stress, anxiety, and negative emotions by staying present and aware of your surroundings. Mindfulness meditation is often practiced by those seeking to improve their mental clarity and overall well-being.

Transcendental meditation:

There is a specific technique of meditation that involves the repetition of a mantra, which can be a word or a phrase, and this repetitive act can be quite helpful in calming the mind and focusing your thoughts. This method can be effective in helping individuals achieve a state of deep relaxation and inner peace, which is why meditation experts often recommend it. By repeating a mantra, you can quiet your mind and let go of any distracting thoughts or worries occupying your attention.

This technique can benefit those who struggle with anxiety or stress as it provides a simple and effective way to reduce tension and improve overall well-being.

Vipassana meditation/Inner Bliss meditation:
In this form of meditation, you focus on observing your thoughts and emotions without discernment. Take note of how your thoughts appear and disappear. Furthermore, by focusing on our thoughts and feelings non-judgmentally, we can cultivate a sense of calm and clarity that can be incredibly valuable as we navigate life's challenges. Rather than reacting impulsively or being overwhelmed by emotions, we can learn to remain centered and grounded, even in adversity.

It's also called mindfulness, inner bliss meditation, a tool that can help us live more fully and authentically by enabling connecting with ourselves and the world around us.

How does meditation work?

While meditation may be considered a modern science, it has been proven to provide many benefits for the mind and body. Scientific research has shown that regular meditation can help reduce stress, lower blood pressure, improve sleep quality, and enhance overall well-being. Additionally, meditation has increased focus, improved memory, and even led to physical changes in the brain that promote emotional regulation and cognitive flexibility.

With all of these benefits, it is no wonder that meditation has become a popular tool for those seeking to improve their mental and physical health.

- **Reduced stress and anxiety:** Meditation can help calm the mind and body, lessening stress and anxiety.
- **Improved focus and concentration:** Meditation can train the mind to focus more and concentrate.
- **Increased self-awareness:** Meditation can help you to become more aware of your thoughts, feelings, and sensations.
- **Enhanced creativity:** Meditation can help to improve creativity and problem-solving skills.
- **Improved sleep quality:** Meditation can help to improve sleep quality by reducing stress and anxiety.

If you are considering meditation, taking the necessary steps to prepare yourself for the activity is crucial. This includes conducting thorough research and familiarizing yourself with the various types of meditation available and the unique benefits that each one provides. By doing so, you will be better equipped to choose the type of meditation that aligns with your personal goals and preferences, and you will be more likely to have a positive and productive meditation experience.

Find a quiet place where you won't be disturbed:

Sometimes, we crave a tranquil and uninterrupted environment to decompress and rejuvenate.

Fortunately, we can effortlessly discover such a haven within the comforts of our abode.

Whether it's our designated bedroom, an unoccupied chamber, or a snug nook in our communal space, we can select a spot to unwind and detach ourselves from the din and diversions of the outside world.

Sit in a comfortable position.

If you find that sitting in a cross-legged position on the floor is causing discomfort, there's no need to be concerned. Other alternatives are available, such as sitting on a chair, couch, or bed. It's crucial to prioritize your comfort and ensure your spine remains straight, regardless of your chosen position. Remember, maintaining proper posture during extended periods of sitting is essential for avoiding discomfort and potential health issues.

Close your eyes and focus on your breath:

I recommend that you focus your attention on your chest movements as you inhale deeply and exhale slowly. Please pay close attention to the sensation of air as it flows in and out of your nostrils. Doing so will help you cultivate a heightened sense of awareness regarding your breath, enabling you to be fully present in the present moment.

If your mind wanders, gently bring it back to your breath:

It's entirely natural for our minds to drift off and lose focus. It's important not to be too harsh on ourselves or get frustrated when this happens. Instead, we can gently redirect our attention to our breath and continue practicing. Remember, mindfulness is a journey, and detaining is alright.

Start with short meditations and gradually increase the length of time:

If you're starting with meditation, let's begin with shorter sessions of about 5 or 10 minutes. To feel more at ease and secure while meditating, it's recommended to start with shorter sessions and gradually increase the duration as you become more familiar with the practice. One can unlock many benefits and elevate their experience through continued dedication to meditation. Remember to take it slow and be patient with yourself as you build your skills.

Be patient and persistent:

Establishing a consistent practice is undeniably crucial when it comes to meditation.

Maintaining the routine requires discipline and patience, even when the results may not seem apparent. However, the positive benefits will eventually manifest as you persevere and become more noticeable. Hence, it is essential to remain committed and persistent in your practice to reap the full potential of its benefits.

Here are some additional tips:

Use a mantra: When engaging in meditation, utilizing a mantra, a word or phrase you repeatedly recite to yourself, can be helpful. This technique assists in maintaining focus and concentration of the mind. By repeating the mantra, one can quiet the chatter of the mind and achieve a state of calm and relaxation.

Listen to guided meditations: The internet and application marketplaces present many options for those seeking guided meditation. These resources serve as an exceptional aid for individuals looking to acquire knowledge of meditation techniques and develop their concentration ability during practice.

Join a meditation group: Making connections with individuals who are passionate about meditation can be a precious experience. Engaging with like-minded practitioners can offer an opportunity to glean insights from their personal journeys and enhance your practice. By engaging with a community of individuals who share a common interest in meditation, you can foster a sense of support and camaraderie that can assist you in maintaining your motivation and dedication toward your practice.

So, don't hesitate to seek out these connections and see how they can enrich your meditation journey.

Consider integrating meditation into your daily routine if you find yourself constantly juggling tasks and responsibilities, experiencing difficulty focusing, or just yearning for a break from the daily grind. This practice has proven to be an effective and valuable tool in promoting relaxation and enhancing mindfulness, allowing you to manage the challenges that may come your way.

However, it's important to remember that the benefits of meditation may take time and require regular practice over time. So, be prepared to commit to a consistent approach and be patient with yourself as you explore this practice. With patience and persistence, you can reap the many benefits of meditation.

If you're looking to start meditating, you'll be pleased to know it's easier than you think. By following these simple steps, you can reap the many benefits of this ancient practice. First, find a quiet and comfortable spot where you won't be disturbed. Sit cross-legged on a cushion or chair with your back straight, and place your hands on your knees. Begin by taking a few deep breaths, then shift your focus to your breath. Observe the sensation of air moving in and out of your nose or mouth, and try to maintain a steady rhythm.

When your mind inevitably wanders, gently bring it back to your breath. Start with just a few minutes a day and gradually increase the length of your sessions. Regular practice makes you feel calmer, more focused, and better handle stress. If you are interested in exploring the practice of meditation, in that case, there are several steps you should take to ensure that you are prepared and able to engage in this activity effectively:

- Acquiring knowledge and researching the numerous types of meditation is a valuable endeavor as the benefits they offer vary greatly. It is highly recommended that individuals take the time to explore the various forms of meditation available and understand their unique advantages to make informed decisions about which practice to incorporate into their daily routine.

- For those seeking to establish a space devoid of disturbances or disruptions, creating a tranquil environment is crucial. Additionally, it's advisable for those seeking to establish consistent meditation practicable to designate a specific time each day for reflection to integrate it seamlessly into their daily routine. Adopting these strategies can ensure a successful meditation practice and reap its numerous benefits.

- It would help to approach meditation with an open and curious mindset, allowing yourself to explore this practice without expectations or judgment.

With these steps in mind, you can begin your journey toward a more mindful and centered way of being.

1. It would help if you found a quiet place where you won't be disturbed.
2. It would help if you sat in a comfortable position where you could keep your spine straight.
3. You need to close your eyes and focus on your breath.

Once you are comfortable, you can begin to practice meditation. You can start by focusing on your breath and gradually add other techniques, such as visualization or meditation. As you practice, you can focus your attention for extended periods and experience a more profound sense of peace and relaxation.

Here are some tips for meditating:

- Start with short meditation sessions of 5-10 minutes and gradually increase the time as you become more comfortable.
- Be patient and consistent with your practice. The benefits of meditation will come with time and practice.
- Find a meditation teacher or group that can support you on your journey.
- Make meditation a part of your daily routine. The more you practice, the more benefits you will experience.

Meditation for beginners:

If you are a beginner to meditation, here are a few tips to help you get started:

- Start by finding a quiet place where you won't be disturbed.
- Sit in a comfortable position where you can keep your spine straight.
- Close your eyes and focus on your breath.
- If your mind wanders, gently bring it back to your breath.
- Start with short meditation sessions of 5-10 minutes and gradually increase the time as you become more comfortable.
- Be patient and consistent with your practice. The benefits of meditation will come with time and practice.

Meditation is a highly recommended technique if you are looking for effective ways to improve your overall physical and mental well-being. This ancient practice has been proven to reduce stress and anxiety levels and enhance concentration and focus, leading to a deeper connection with your inner self. So, why take a step toward a healthier and happier life by incorporating meditation into your routine and experiencing its positive effects?

Meditation is a powerful tool that can help reduce stress, improve focus, and connect with your inner self. Meditation may be a good option if you want to enhance your well-being.

Vipassana meditation/Inner Bliss meditation

Throughout my life, I have faced various challenges that have tested my mental and emotional fortitude. However, I have found solace in practicing Vipassana, or inner bliss meditation. By cultivating a more profound self-awareness through this technique, I have better understood my thoughts, emotions, and actions. Through consistent practice, Vipassana enables me to live more mindfully and with greater intention, allowing me to navigate life's obstacles with greater ease and grace.

Obtaining a sense of inner peace and achieving overall well-being is an aspiration that many individuals strive for. However, the challenges of daily life can often make it difficult to maintain this state of mind. Fortunately, with the help of Inner Bliss Meditation, one can discover an effective solution to alleviate stress and anxiety.

Inner Bliss Meditation is a practice that enables individuals to reduce their stress levels and develop a heightened sense of focus. By incorporating this practice into their daily routine, individuals can gain the ability to manage their emotions and thoughts more effectively. Additionally, Inner Bliss Meditation can help individuals establish a more profound connection with their inner selves, leading to a more fulfilling and meaningful life.

Through Vipassana/Inner Bliss Meditation, individuals can learn to quiet their minds and focus on the present moment. This practice involves deep breathing and visualization techniques, which can help individuals achieve a state of calmness and relaxation. With regular practice, individuals can cultivate a greater sense of inner peace and well-being.

Overall, Vipassana/Inner Bliss Meditation is a valuable tool that can help individuals overcome the challenges of stress and anxiety. By incorporating this practice into their daily routine, individuals can experience a greater sense of calmness, focus, and inner harmony. Without further delay, let's explore the Vipassana/Inner Bliss Meditation.

What is Vipassana meditation/Inner Bliss Meditation?

Inner Bliss Meditation is a type of meditation that is designed to help you achieve a state of inner peace and well-being. It combines different meditation techniques, including focusing on the breath, visualization, and mantra meditation. Inner Bliss Meditation aims to help you connect with your inner self and experience a sense of deep relaxation and joy.

History of Vipassana meditation/inner bliss meditation:

Inner Bliss Meditation is a relatively new type of meditation but it is based on ancient meditation techniques from different traditions, including Buddhism, Hinduism, and Taoism. The practice of Inner Bliss Meditation was developed by Ariadne Kapsali, a meditation teacher and author. Kapsali has been teaching meditation for over 20 years and has developed a unique approach to meditation that is both effective and accessible.

How does Vipassana Meditation/Inner Bliss Meditation Work?

The practice of Inner Bliss Meditation serves as a valuable tool for individuals seeking to alleviate stress and anxiety. Its primary purpose lies in directing attention toward the present moment, allowing one to let go of any thoughts or emotions that may be causing mental or emotional discomfort. By focusing on one's breath, individuals can effectively center themselves, bringing their minds back to the present moment and cultivating a sense of calmness and relaxation throughout their body and mind.

Inner Bliss Meditation involves effectively using visualization as a critical tool. By intentionally imagining a peaceful and calming environment within your mind's eye, you can effectively detach yourself from the overwhelming demands of everyday life. This method aids in promoting a deep sense of relaxation, reducing stress levels, and facilitating a profound connection with your inner self.

Inner Bliss Meditation is centered around the highly effective technique of mantra meditation. This involves repeating a specific word or phrase to facilitate a deep and focused state of mind, ultimately leading to feelings of tranquility and inner peace. Through the power of concentration on a single sound or word, the mind and body can achieve a state of clarity and stillness that is highly beneficial for overall well-being.

Inner Bliss Meditation is an excellent tool for those seeking to cultivate a greater sense of calm and balance in their daily lives.

If you're interested in cultivating inner peace and tranquility, consider exploring the practice of Inner Bliss

Meditation. This form of meditation is designed to help you connect with your inner self and tap into a more profound sense of calm and well-being. Through regular practice, Inner Bliss Meditation can help you reduce stress, boost your immune system, improve your focus and concentration, and enhance your overall sense of happiness and well-being.

Whether new to meditation or a seasoned practitioner, Inner Bliss Meditation can be a powerful tool for improving your physical, mental, and emotional health. So why not see the many benefits this practice can offer? There are many benefits to practicing Inner Bliss Meditation. Some of the benefits include:

1. It has been observed that engaging in certain activities and practices can lead to a noticeable reduction in both stress and anxiety levels. These activities could include anything from meditation and exercise to spending time in nature or engaging in creative pursuits. By incorporating such practices into one's daily routine, it is possible to experience a significant improvement in overall physical well-being and mental health.

2. One of the benefits of using this product is the enhanced ability to focus and concentrate. By utilizing its advanced features, users can expect to experience heightened levels of mental clarity and increased productivity. Whether you're a student studying for exams or a professional working on an important project, this tool can help you stay on track and accomplish your goals with ease.

So, if you want to boost your cognitive abilities and take your performance to the next level, this is the perfect solution.

If you're feeling drained and lacking in energy, there are several steps you can take to give yourself a much-needed boost. From incorporating regular exercise and a balanced diet into your routine to getting enough sleep and staying hydrated throughout the day, focusing on your health and well-being can help you feel more energized and refreshed. Making small changes to your daily habits and prioritizing self-care can improve your energy levels and enjoy a more vibrant, active lifestyle.

3. If you're having trouble getting a good night's sleep, there are several things you can do to improve the quality of your sleep. First, establish a regular sleep schedule by going to bed and waking up at the same time every day. This helps regulate your body's internal clock and can improve the overall quality of your sleep. Also, create a relaxing bedtime routine that lets you wind down before sleep.

   This could include taking a warm bath, reading a book, or practicing relaxation techniques like deep breathing or meditation. It's also essential to ensure your sleeping environment is comfortable and conducive. This means keeping the room cool, dark, and quiet, and investing in comfortable mattresses and pillows. Finally, be mindful of your daytime habits affecting your sleep, such as caffeine intake, exercise, and screen time.

By making minor changes to your daily routine and prioritizing good sleep habits, you can improve your sleep quality and wake up refreshed and energized.

4. Elevate your level of self-awareness and cultivate a more profound sense of mindfulness through enhancements. These tools and techniques can assist you in better understanding your thoughts, emotions, and behaviors, allowing you to make more intentional choices and live a more fulfilling life. By tapping into your inner wisdom and utilizing these resources, you can unlock your true potential and achieve greater peace and happiness.

Engaging in inner bliss meditation regularly can profoundly impact one's emotional well-being. By focusing inward and cultivating a sense of calm and tranquility, individuals may experience heightened feelings of joy and contentment, leading to a greater understanding of fulfillment and satisfaction. This practice can be a powerful tool for promoting overall mental health and happiness.

How to practice Vipassana meditation/inner bliss meditation:
If you wish to experience the benefits of Inner Bliss Meditation, then here are some easy steps to follow. Firstly, try to find a peaceful spot to meditate without any disturbances. This could be in your home, garden, or a quiet outdoor location. Secondly, sit comfortably on a cushion or chair with your spine straight and your feet firmly on the ground. You may also choose to cross your legs in a lotus position. Finally, close your eyes and focus on your breath.

Inhale slowly and deeply, feel your lungs expand, exhale slowly, and feel your body relax. Continue to concentrate on your breathing and try to clear your mind of any thoughts that may arise.

With consistent practice, the benefits of Inner Bliss Meditation can be genuinely transformative. Not only can it help to alleviate stress but it can also lead to an increased sense of focus and inner peace. As you become more comfortable with the practice, you may explore various techniques to enhance your experience.

One effective start method is focusing on your breath and gradually adding visualization and mantra meditation. Inner Bliss Meditation can help you achieve deeper self-awareness and overall well-being with time and dedication.

As you continue to devote time and effort toward honing your ability to focus, you can sustain your attention for extended periods. This newfound skill will enable you to fully immerse yourself in the present moment, fostering a greater sense of serenity and tranquility.

Conclusion

Discovering a sense of inner peace and overall well-being can be a challenging task, but with the help of Inner Bliss Meditation, it becomes achievable. This practice offers an effective solution for individuals struggling with stress and anxiety, allowing them to reduce their stress levels and develop a heightened sense of focus. Additionally, Inner Bliss Meditation can help individuals establish a more profound connection with their inner selves, enabling them to lead a more fulfilling and meaningful life.

Here are some additional tips for practicing Vipassana meditation/Inner Bliss Meditation:

- Start with short meditation sessions of 5-10 minutes and gradually increase the time as you become more comfortable.
- Be patient and consistent with your practice. The benefits of meditation will come with time and practice.
- Find a meditation teacher or group that can support you on your journey.
- Make meditation a part of your daily routine. The more you practice, the more benefits you will experience.

Chapter 3: Yoga

What is yoga?

Yoga, an ancient Indian practice with a history spanning 5,000 years, involves a combination of physical postures, breathing exercises, and meditation or relaxation techniques. This holistic approach to wellness has numerous styles, each with unique benefits and practices. Whether you prefer a gentle, restorative method or a vigorous, athletic one, yoga can meet your needs and help you achieve your wellness goals.

With its emphasis on mindfulness and self-awareness, inner yoga is an excellent way to improve physical and mental health while cultivating a more profound connection to yourself and the world around you.

The term "yoga" can be traced back to ancient India, specifically to the Sanskrit word "yuj". This term translates to "to yoke" or "to unite", reflecting the yoga philosophy. According to this philosophy, the mind and body are not separate entities but are interconnected. Yoga aims to bring these two aspects together and create balance and harmony. By practicing yoga, individuals can improve their physical, mental, and spiritual well-being and cultivate greater self-awareness and inner peace.

Practicing Yoga has evolved but some common elements are found in all styles of yoga. These include:

Physical postures:

The yoga practice comprises various poses referred to as asanas. These asanas are meticulously crafted to promote and enhance the body's strength and flexibility while reducing stress and improving balance. By incorporating these postures into a regular yoga practice, individuals can attain a more profound and holistic approach to physical and mental well-being.

Breathing exercises:

Pranayama, which can be defined as the practice of yoga breathing exercises, is a technique that focuses on regulating breathing patterns. The ultimate goal of this practice is to improve circulation, boost energy levels, and enhance mental focus. This technique involves a series of breathing exercises designed to increase awareness of one's breath and its relationship with the body. By practicing pranayama regularly, individuals can experience many benefits that positively impact their health and well-being.

Meditation or relaxation:

Yoga encompasses various techniques that promote mental and physical health. One such technique is meditation, which can help to calm the mind and promote inner tranquility. Additionally, Yoga incorporates relaxation techniques that can reduce stress and promote overall well-being. It is worth noting that several styles of yoga have unique focal points and methods. Individuals can find the best approach to their needs and goals by exploring different types.

What are the different types of yoga?

When it comes yoga, there are plenty of options. Many practitioners have a few favorite styles that they stick to but there are countless variations and hybrids to explore. The most commonly practiced type of yoga includes Hatha, Vinyasa, Ashtanga, Bikram, and Restorative. Each style has its unique focus, pace, and set of poses, so it's worth trying out a few to see what resonates with you the most. Yoga is perfect whether you're looking to build strength, improve flexibility, reduce stress, or find inner peace.

Hatha Yoga:

"Physical yoga" describes any style that focuses primarily on practicing and mastering physical postures or asanas. Rather than focusing on meditation or breathwork, physio-yoga emphasizes improving flexibility, strength, and balance through a series of challenging poses. Many types of physio-yoga exist, each with unique postures and techniques.

Vinyasa Yoga:

This yoga is a practice that centers around the synchronization of breath and movement. This type of Yoga prioritizes the connection between these two elements, encouraging practitioners to move mindfully and intentionally with each inhale and exhale. Through this mindful approach to movement and breath, individuals can cultivate a more profound sense of presence and awareness within their bodies and minds.

Ashtanga Yoga:

This particular yoga entails a high-energy and intense approach, concentrating on executing a prearranged sequence of various yoga postures.

Iyeyoga Yoga: Practice yoga offers many styles and techniques, one of which is known for its emphasis on precision and correct body positioning in different postures. This style strives for alignment accuracy, ensuring that each pose has the proper form and technique for maximum benefits.

Bikram Yoga:

Hot or Biyoga Yoga requires practicing in a heated room with temperatures ranging from 95 to 108 degrees Fahrenheit. This type of yoga involves a series of twenty-six postures and two breathing exercises, all of which are designed to enhance flexibility, strength, and balance. The high temperature promotes sweating, detoxification, and increased blood flow. Yoga is popular for those seeking a challenging and invigorating workout.

Kundalini Yoga:

Kundalini yoga is a unique practice that combines physical movements, regulated breathing techniques, and vocalization to stimulate the awakening of one's spiritual potential. This yoga has many benefits, including a boost in energy levels, enhanced mental clarity and focus, lower stress levels, heightened intuition, and even spiritual growth. As a holistic approach to wellness, Kundalini yoga provides practitioners a powerful tool for achieving balance and harmony in mind and body.

Yin Yoga:

Yin yoga is a highly beneficial style known for its slow-paced movements and extended periods of holding poses. This practice is designed to enhance flexibility and promote inner stillness, making it an excellent choice for those looking to improve their physical and mental well-being. By practicing yin yoga, individuals can experience various benefits, including increased flexibility and range of motion, reduced stress levels, increased energy, enhanced mental clarity, and improved sleep quality.

With its focus on deep relaxation and gentle, sustained stretching, yin yoga is a beautiful way to promote overall health and wellness.

Restorative Yoga:

Restorative yoga focuses on passive poses and utilizes different props, such as blankets, blocks, and bolsters, to aid the body in holding the poses for extended periods. This yoga is gentle, soothing, and perfect for those who want to relax and unwind. The benefits of Restorative Yoga include reducing stress levels, promoting relaxation, improving sleep quality, enhancing mental clarity and concentration, increasing circulation, and reducing pain and tension in the body.

By regularly practicing Restorative Yoga, individuals can experience a greater sense of calmness, reduced anxiety, and overall physical and mental well-being.

Yoga is a safe and effective practice for people of all ages and fitness levels. However, it is essential to start slowly and gradually increase the intensity of your course. Talk to your doctor before beginning yoga if you have any health concerns. The history of yoga is long and complex. The earliest evidence of yoga practice can be found in the Rig Veda, a collection of sacred hymns that date back to 1500 BCE. However, it is believed that yoga practices may have originated even earlier.

Over the century, yoga has undergone significant evolution and development, becoming a worldwide phenomenon millions engage in for physical and mental health benefits. The Yoga Sutras of Patanjali, written around the 2nd century BCE, are widely recognized as the definitive source of yoga philosophy and practice. Yoga's influence has spread to various parts of the world, including China, Tibet, and Southeast Asia while gaining immense popularity in the West during the 20th century.

Nowadays, yoga is a highly valued form of exercise and relaxation that has been shown to provide numerous benefits for practitioners. These benefits include improvements in physical health, such as increased flexibility, strength, and balance, as well as mental health benefits, like reduced stress, anxiety, and depression. Yoga is also known to lower blood pressure and improve cardiovascular health, making it an excellent practice for individuals with heart health concerns.

Yoga has proven to be a highly effective way to promote overall wellness and maintain a healthy body and mind.

- Improved flexibility and strength
- Reduced stress and anxiety

- Improved balance and coordination
- Increased energy levels
- Improved sleep quality
- Reduced pain
- Increased self-awareness
- Improved mental clarity
- Enhanced spiritual well-being

Many resources are available if you are interested in learning more about yoga. You can find yoga classes in most cities, and many books and websites can teach you yoga. Yoga is a safe and effective way to improve physical and mental health. It is a practice that people of all ages and fitness levels can enjoy. If you want to do yoga, please try a class in your area. You may be surprised at how much you enjoy it.

When it comes to yoga, there are a plethora of options available to choose from. You must experiment with various types to determine the best fit for your unique needs and preferences.

You will experience the incredible benefits of this time-honored practice, whether Hatha, Vinyasa, or any other style. So, why start your yoga journey today and experience its transformative power for yourself?

Practicing yoga offers a variety of styles, each with its unique focus and benefits. Regular yoga has numerous advantages, including increased flexibility, strength, balance, reduced stress, and improved sleep quality. Regardless of age or fitness, yoga is a versatile exercise form that anyone can practice. You can find a suitable yoga class online, at a nearby studio, or home. Incorporating yoga into your lifestyle is an excellent way to enhance your overall health and well-being.

How to do yoga?

Depending on your preference and lifestyle, there are many ways to practice yoga. You can attend classes at local gyms and studios or take advantage of the convenience of online sessions. Alternatively, you can create your yoga sanctuary in the comfort of your home. Starting with a beginner's class is recommended for novices as it introduces you to the fundamental poses and breathing techniques.

Practicing in a group environment also allows for learning from others and receiving guidance from an experienced instructor. Once you have established a solid foundation, you can continue to hone your skills with resources such as yoga DVDs and online tutorials. These tools allow you to practice at your own pace and in the comfort of your own space.

If you're a newbie to the world of yoga, it's essential to take things at a comfortable pace and listen to your body. It doesn't matter which type of yoga you opt for, but attending a class led by a certified yoga instructor is highly recommended. You can learn proper techniques and avoid injuries from incorrect postures or movements. Starting with a certified instructor also provides the foundation for a long-term yoga practice which can help you attain physical, mental, and emotional benefits.

If you're interested in incorporating yoga into your daily routine and practicing in the comfort of your home, there are a few helpful tips to remember. Firstly, it's essential to create a designated space for your practice, free from distractions and clutter. You should also invest in a good-quality yoga mat to ensure safety and comfort during poses. Additionally, plenty of online resources are available for guided yoga classes and tutorials, which can be a great way to learn and improve your practice.

Listen to your body, take breaks when needed, and consult a healthcare professional before starting any new exercise routine. With these tips in mind, you'll be well on your way to fulfilling and enjoyable yoga practice at home.

Conducting thorough research and identifying the available types is crucial when practicing yoga. Every kind of yoga offers unique benefits and caters to specific needs, so it's essential to find the one that best suits your requirements. By selecting the proper type of yoga, you can ensure that you reap the maximum benefits and achieve your desired outcomes. Once you decide on the type of yoga:

- When starting your yoga practice, choosing a location where you feel comfortable and at ease is essential. Remember to grab a yoga mat to provide a stable surface to move on, and consider having a towel or blanket nearby for added comfort and support during your practice. Ensuring you have the right environment and equipment can help you get the most out of your yoga routine.

- Opting for clothing that is not overly tight and provides ample room for unhindered movement is highly recommended. This will ensure maximum comfort and flexibility, especially during physical activities or tasks that require a wide range of motion. It is essential to prioritize style and functionality when selecting clothing to balance looking good and feeling comfortable.

- To start your yoga journey, it is recommended to begin with basic poses that are easy to execute. These poses will help you get comfortable with the movements and breathing techniques commonly used in yoga. As you progress in your practice, you can gradually move on to more advanced poses that require greater flexibility and strength.

  Always listen to your body and never push yourself beyond your limits. You'll soon achieve new physical and mental wellness levels with consistency and dedication through yoga.

- If you encounter any form of physical discomfort while performing a yoga pose, it is highly advised to discontinue the posture and rest briefly immediately fly. This will help alleviate discomfort or pain and ensure you remain safe throughout your yoga practice. Remember, it is always better to prioritize your well-being over pushing yourself too hard in a particular pose.

- Taking deep breaths and focusing on your body when moving from one posture to another is helpful. This can aid in maintaining a sense of calm and stability during the transition. Paying attention to your breath and physical sensations can also ensure that you are moving safely and with proper alignment. Remember to take time and tune in to your body's needs as you flow through your practice.

- As you end your practice session, allowing yourself a few moments to unwind and relax is essential. Take time to clear your mind and release any tension or stress that may have built up during your practice. This will help you feel more centered and grounded and allow you to carry the benefits of your course throughout the rest of your day. So take a deep breath, let go of any concerns or distractions, and allow yourself to be present in the moment.

- Partaking in regular yoga practice can provide you with an opportunity to decompress and indulge in moments of relaxation and enjoyment. Yoga's meditative and physical aspects can help you release tension and stress while promoting overall well-being and inner peace. If you want to prioritize your mental and physical health, incorporating yoga into your routine is worthwhile.

Yoga is a great way to improve your physical and mental health. It is a safe and effective exercise for people of all ages and fitness levels. Starting slowly and listening to your body is a good idea if you are doing yoga. With regular practice, you will soon experience the many benefits of yoga.

Benefits of yoga for accessing bliss

There are numerous benefits of incorporating yoga into your daily routine. Not only does it promote physical fitness and flexibility, but it also has been shown to reduce stress and anxiety levels. Additionally, practicing yoga can improve overall mental health and increase mindfulness. The advantages of regularly practicing yoga are numerous and can significantly improve one's overall well-being.

Reduces stress and anxiety:

Yoga is a popular activity with numerous benefits, particularly reducing stress levels. The practice involves focusing on the present moment, letting go of negative thoughts and emotions, and achieving a state of tranquility. Combining physical movements with breathing exercises, yoga helps individuals gain a sense of calmness and relaxation, which can positively impact both the mind and body.

Whether you're a beginner or an experienced practitioner, incorporating yoga into your daily routine can significantly improve your overall well-being and reduce the harmful effects of stress.

Improves flexibility and range of motion:

Regularly engaging in yoga poses is an effective way to stretch and strengthen your muscles and joints. This can significantly improve your flexibility and range of motion, which in turn can dramatically reduce the likelihood of sustaining injuries. Additionally, these benefits make your daily activities feel much more manageable overall. Therefore, incorporating yoga into your fitness routine can benefit your physical health.

Builds strength and endurance:

Engaging in regular yoga practice can have a significant impact on your physical strength and endurance. Yoga involves holding various poses for extended periods, which requires much muscle engagement and stability. You can gradually increase your overall strength and endurance levels by consistently challenging your muscles, leading to a healthier, more resilient body.

Improves balance and coordination:

Engaging in regular yoga practice can significantly improve your balance and coordination abilities. Yoga entails holding different poses that require you to coordinate your movements while maintaining your balance. This means that with consistent yoga practice, your body learns to control and stabilize itself, enhancing balance and coordination skills.

Promotes better sleep:

Incorporating a regular yoga practice into your lifestyle has the potential to significantly improve the quality of your sleep. Yoga's calming effects on the mind and body can help reduce stress levels and promote relaxation. By focusing on deep breathing and gentle movement, yoga can help to release tension and encourage a more profound understanding of inner peace. This can lead to more restful and rejuvenating sleep, allowing you to wake up refreshed and energized each morning.

Boosts energy levels:

Regular practicing yoga has been scientifically proven to positively impact energy levels. Yoga enhances circulation throughout the body, allowing for more excellent oxygen and nutrient delivery to the cells. Additionally, yoga promotes the production of endorphins, the body's natural feel-good chemicals. These endorphins help reduce stress and improve mood, increasing energy and vitality. Therefore, incorporating yoga into your daily routine can be a powerful tool for boosting your overall health and well-being.

Improves overall health and well-being:

Engaging in regular yoga sessions can tremendously benefit your physical and mental health. Besides improving your flexibility, yoga can also enhance your strength, decrease stress levels, and promote better sleep quality. Consistently doing yoga can be a holistic approach to overall wellness and vitality.

How does yoga help you access bliss?

Yoga has been proven to offer numerous benefits, one of the most notable being attaining a state of pure bliss. This state is marked by a profound sense of peace, joy, and overall well-being, unencumbered by the stresses of anxiety, physical discomfort, and other burdens. Through various techniques, yoga offers individuals diverse pathways to attain bliss, ultimately leading to a more enriching and fulfilling life experience.

Yoga is a holistic practice that offers several pathways to reaching a state of bliss. One of the most effective approaches is through physical postures, or asanas, which can help to alleviate tension and stress in both the body and mind. The body becomes more relaxed and flexible by stretching and strengthening the muscles, while the mind becomes calmer and more centered.

Another critical component of yoga is the practice of pranayama, or breathing exercises.

These techniques can enhance oxygen flow to the brain, improving cognitive function and promoting feelings of happiness and well-being. Learning to control your breath allows you to regulate your thoughts and emotions, leading to greater inner peace and harmony.

Finally, incorporating meditation practices into your yoga routine can be a powerful way to cultivate inner peace. Meditation involves focusing on the present moment, letting go of distractions and worries, and connecting with a more profound sense of consciousness. Through regular meditation, you can develop greater clarity of mind, heightened awareness, and a greater capacity for compassion and empathy toward yourself and others.

Overall, yoga is a transformative practice that can help you find more balance, harmony, and joy.

Physiological effects of yoga:

Practicing yoga is known for its myriad physiological benefits that contribute to physical and mental well-being. One of the most notable advantages is its ability to reduce stress levels by lowering cortisol, the hormone responsible for stress. This reduction in pressure can lead to improved sleep quality by reducing anxiety and promoting relaxation.

Moreover, yoga has been proven to increase energy levels by improving circulation and metabolism, which can help individuals feel more alert and focused throughout the day. Practicing yoga regularly can help reduce pain by increasing flexibility and strength while improving circulation. Finally, it's worth noting that yoga can improve cardiovascular health by lowering blood pressure, heart rate, and cholesterol levels. With so many benefits, it's no wonder yoga has become an increasingly popular form of exercise and relaxation.

Psychological effects of yoga:

Incorporating yoga into your routine can offer many psychological advantages to your overall well-being. One of the most significant benefits is the heightened self-awareness of observing your thoughts and emotions without judgment. This newfound self-awareness can help you better understand your feelings and thought patterns, leading to a more profound knowledge of yourself.

Furthermore, yoga is known for reducing stress and anxiety, promoting happiness, and boosting mood. Regular practice teaches you to release negative emotions and embrace the present moment, leading to a more positive outlook.

Additionally, yoga can enhance mental clarity by teaching you how to focus your mind and eliminate distractions, facilitating better decision-making and increased productivity. Moreover, yoga can teach you relaxation techniques that promote a sense of tranquility and calmness, helping to reduce anxiety. Finally, and most importantly, practicing yoga can elevate your self-esteem by teaching you how to accept yourself and cultivate a stronger sense of self-worth and self-confidence.

Practicing yoga can help you reduce stress and promote relaxation. Focusing on your breath and body can quiet your mind and release tension. This sense of calmness can lead to a blissful experience.

In addition to relaxation, Yoga can also help you connect with your body. As you become more aware of your body and its sensations, you can cultivate appreciation and peace. This connection can also contribute to a blissful state.

Through yoga, you can develop a sense of inner peace by focusing on the present moment. This mindfulness can help you let go of worries about the past or future and promote a sense of contentment. This sense of inner peace can also contribute to a blissful experience.

Finally, yoga can help you cultivate gratitude by increasing awareness of the good things in your life. Being present and appreciative of the present moment can make you feel more grateful and promote a sense of joy and bliss.

How to access bliss through yoga:

Yoga is a discipline that offers various means to reach a state of complete happiness and satisfaction, often known as bliss. Below are some highly effective techniques that can be employed to attain this state of bliss.

To truly access the transformative power of yoga, make it a regular part of your life.

Experts recommend practicing for at least three to five sessions per week, each lasting between 30 minutes to an hour. As you begin your journey, focusing on your breath is essential, allowing it to guide you through each pose and calm your mind. Remember to tune into your body, respecting its limits and avoiding the temptation to push yourself too hard too soon.

If you feel discomfort or pain, pause the pose and take a break. This will help prevent any injuries and allow you to progress at a safe and steady pace. Remember, yoga is a lifelong practice that requires patience, discipline, and persistence. As you continue to commit yourself to this beautiful discipline, you will begin to experience the incredible euphoria and exhilaration that comes with the territory.

Conclusion

Yoga is a powerful tool that can help you access bliss. Yoga is an excellent option to reconnect with your body and experience peace. Just start practicing regularly and be patient. With time and practice, you will eventually experience bliss.

In addition to the benefits mentioned above, practicing yoga regularly can provide other advantages. For instance, it can lead to a better quality of sleep, which can help alleviate various sleep disorders. Furthermore, it can also help reduce pain, which is especially beneficial for those suffering from arthritis or chronic back pain. Additionally, yoga has been shown to increase energy levels, improve mood, and enhance cognitive function, making it an ideal choice for those looking to boost their overall well-being.

Finally, regular yoga practice has also been linked to a decreased risk of chronic diseases such as heart disease, diabetes, and cancer. Overall, the benefits of yoga are varied, making it a worthwhile activity for anyone seeking to improve their physical and mental health.

Yoga is widely renowned for its safety and efficacy, making it an ideal practice for individuals of all ages and fitness levels. One can begin practicing yoga by attending classes at a reputable gym or studio or, alternatively, by utilizing the vast array of online resources available for practicing in the comfort of one's home. Regardless of the chosen method, the benefit of yoga is plentiful and can significantly improve one's physical and mental well-being.

Upon completing this chapter, you will fully comprehend the beneficial impact yoga has on accessing a state of bliss. This ancient practice has been shown to drastically enhance physical and mental health, making it an outstanding option for individuals seeking to improve their overall well-being. It is imperative to note that consistent and patient practice is critical as the benefit of yoga may require time to manifest fully. However, one can eventually attain a state of bliss with a dedicated and disciplined approach.

Chapter 4: Spending Time in Nature

Why is spending time in nature important?
Throughout history, humans have established a deep bond with nature, recognizing its pivotal role in physical and mental health. Nevertheless, in the present era, we have become increasingly disconnected from the natural world as we tend to spend more hours confined indoors and have fewer chances to engage with it. This shift in lifestyle has been associated with several negative consequences, such as a rise in stress levels, a decline in cognitive function, and an increase in chronic illnesses.

Therefore, we must acknowledge the importance of nature in our lives and take steps to reconnect with it.

There is no denying that our physical and mental well-being has been severely affected due to our growing disconnection from nature. Recent research has shown that individuals spend considerable time in nature. Individuals who have this experience tend to have much lower levels of stress, anxiety, and depression. Moreover, such individuals tend to have more robust immune systems, better quality of sleep, and lower blood pressure.

Therefore, it is essential that we consciously make an effort to include nature in our daily routine as much as possible so that we can reap its numerous benefits.

Apart from the physical advantages of spending time in nature, we can derive numerous mental and emotional benefits. Nature's tranquility and serenity can significantly alleviate stress and anxiety and improve our overall mood and well-being. Taking a break from our busy lives and immersing ourselves in nature can also help us unwind and recharge our batteries.

Additionally, being surrounded by natural beauty can help us establish a deeper connection with ourselves and the people around us, allowing us to be more present at the moment and appreciate the simple things in life.

Nature offers many opportunities for individuals to indulge in its beauty and tranquility. From a leisurely stroll in the park to an invigorating hike in the woods, there are many ways to immerse oneself in the great outdoors. Simply basking in the serenity of one's backyard and inhaling the crisp, fresh air can also do wonders for one's health and overall well-being. Indeed, the benefits of spending time in nature are plentiful and should be considered.

Numerous benefits to spending time in nature should be noted. Not only does it provide a break from the hustle and bustle of everyday life, but it can also improve physical and mental health. Studies have shown that being in nature can reduce stress levels, lower blood pressure, and boost the immune system. Additionally, it can increase creativity, improve focus, and promote overall mood.

Furthermore, spending time in nature allows for a greater appreciation of the environment and can lead to a desire to protect and preserve natural resources. Overall, there are many compelling reasons to spend more time in nature.

Reduces stress:

Research has shown that spending time in natural environments can positively impact our mental health and well-being. Specifically, being surrounded by nature has been found to help lower cortisol levels, a hormone associated with stress. In addition, spending time in nature has been shown to improve our ability to cope with stress, which can have long-term benefits for our overall health.

Whether going for a hike, taking a walk in the park, or simply sitting outside and enjoying the scenery, connecting with nature can be a powerful tool for managing stress and improving our quality of life.

Improves mood:

If you're feeling down or struggling with depression and anxiety, spending time in nature can be a powerful way to lift your mood. Studies have shown that being surrounded by nature can stimulate the production of essential neurotransmitters like serotonin and dopamine, which can help alleviate symptoms and promote well-being.

Whether you walk in the woods, spend time in a park, or simply sit outside and soak up the sun, spending time in nature can be a simple but effective way to boost your mood and improve your mental health.

Boosts creativity:

Taking a break from the hustle and bustle of daily life to spend time in nature has been found to positively impact creativity. By immersing oneself in natural surroundings and being away from the distractions of technology and urban environments, the mind can think more clearly and come up with fresh perspectives. This can lead to developing innovative ideas and solutions to challenges and providing a sense of calm and relaxation. So, if you're feeling stuck or need inspiration, consider going to the great outdoors.

Improves sleep quality:

Spending a few moments amidst the serenity of nature can work wonders in enhancing the quality of our sleep. This is primarily because a character has a calming effect on our senses, allowing us to relax and unwind before hitting the bed. Moreover, it also helps regulate our circadian rhythm, an intrinsic sleep-wake cycle that dictates when we should sleep and wake up. Therefore, incorporating some natural elements into our bedtime routine can immensely benefit our well-being.

Strengthens the immune system:

Engaging in outdoor activities and spending time in nature can positively affect our health. One of the most significant benefits is boosting our immune system through exposure to beneficial bacteria and viruses in the natural environment. Additionally, spending time in nature has been shown to reduce inflammation, a major contributing factor to many chronic diseases. We can improve our overall health and well-being by incorporating time outdoors into our daily routine.

Low blood pressure:

Engaging in outdoor activities and spending time in natural environments can significantly benefit your overall well-being. Studies have shown that exposure to nature can effectively reduce stress levels, improving heart health and decreasing the risk of heart disease and stroke. Therefore, incorporating nature into your daily routine can be an excellent way to promote a healthier and happier lifestyle.

Different ways to spend time in nature

If you intend to spend some time in nature, consider a few tips to guarantee your experience is gratifying and secure. If you're looking for ways to enjoy the beauty of nature, here are some suggestions:

Go for a walk in the park:

Engaging in a leisurely stroll through the serene ambiance of a garden not only serves as a means of physical exercise but also offers the added benefit of inhaling the refreshing scent of nature. This activity is undoubtedly a universal source of enjoyment for all individuals.

Hiking in the woods:

Engaging in this particular activity may demand a greater exertion of physical energy, yet the rewards are immeasurable since it presents an exclusive chance to establish a deeper connection with the environment.

Sit in your backyard:

Despite limited space constraints, one can still find solace in nature by simply stepping into their backyard and immersing themselves in the soft, melodious chirping of the birds. The therapeutic effects of listening to these sweet melodies cannot be overstated as they can soothe the soul and ease the mind, even during a bustling urban environment. So, take a moment to sit back, relax, and appreciate the beauty of the natural world that surrounds you, no matter how small or confined your backyard may be.

Visit a botanical garden:

Exploring the vast array of plants and flowers presents a unique chance to gain insight into each species' diverse characteristics and qualities. By delving deeper into botany, one can develop a deeper appreciation for the intricacies of nature and the fascinating processes that govern the growth and development of these living organisms. Whether you are a seasoned gardener or a curious observer, there is always something new and exciting to discover in plant life.

Camping:

Participating in camping provides a unique and unparalleled opportunity to disconnect from the fast-paced and demanding routine of everyday life and fully immerse oneself in the awe-inspiring wonders of the natural world. This adventure is an excellent way to flee the anxiety-inducing pressures of city living and revel in the tranquility and breathtaking beauty of the great outdoors.

Gardening:

Engaging in this endeavor offers many advantages, such as upholding a robust and energetic routine, all while surrounded by the tranquil splendor of the great outdoors.

Moreover, it allows cultivating and reaping the rewards of freshly grown crops, a gratifying and economical experience.

Individuals should prioritize regularly setting aside a specific time to fully engage with the natural world. Whether one prefers to embark on a scenic walk, take a challenging hike, or simply sit and appreciate the serene surroundings, the benefits of spending quality time in nature are boundless and immeasurable. The longer one dedicates to immersing oneself in nature, the more profound the positive impact on physical and mental well-being will become.

Conclusively, dedicating a portion of your valuable time to immersing yourself in nature's tranquil and awe-inspiring beauty can profoundly impact your physical and mental health. This simple yet fulfilling activity can bring a sense of serenity and tranquility that can work wonders in alleviating stress and anxiety.

The compelling argument presented in this essay underscores the importance of prioritizing time in nature as a critical element in enhancing your overall well-being. If you are seeking to elevate your health and well-being, please make it a priority to spend time in nature. This decision is sure to bring about immense satisfaction and fulfillment.

Benefits of spending time in nature for accessing bliss

Throughout history, individuals have been drawn to the natural world's serene, harmonious, and captivating essence. As of late, researchers have unearthed a plethora of physical and psychological advantages that come with spending time in nature. Multiple studies have shown that immersing oneself in nature can reduce stress levels, boost overall mood, stimulate creativity, and extend one's lifespan.

One of the most significant benefits of spending time in nature is attaining a state of pure bliss. This state is characterized by a profound sense of happiness, tranquility, and overall wellness, where we feel entirely in sync with ourselves, those around us, and the surrounding natural environment. There's nothing quite like the sensation of being completely connected to the world in this way, which everyone should strive to experience at least once in their lifetime.

There are numerous ways to immerse oneself in the sheer delight of nature. One can opt for hiking, camping, or gardening, prevalent activities that provide great joy and contentment. On the other hand, some people prefer to meditate and bask in the serene beauty of the natural surroundings, taking in the picturesque vistas, melodious sounds, and sweet fragrances that abound. Regardless of the choice, nature provides endless happiness and tranquility for those who seek it.

Discover how nature can enhance bliss from within.

Numerous factors make being in nature a conducive environment for experiencing a sense of tranquility and contentment. One of the most prominent reasons is the inherent serenity that the character exudes. The soft melodies of birds singing, the gentle rustle of leaves as the wind blows through the trees, and the refreshing breeze that brushes against your skin all work together to create a calming atmosphere that can effectively alleviate feelings of stress and anxiety.

Moreover, it is undeniable that nature is replete with an inexhaustible array of aesthetically pleasing features. From the vivid colors of a sunset to the intricate patterns of a butterfly's wings, the natural world is a veritable treasure trove of visual delights. Such captivating sights can be a source of profound inspiration, evoking a sense of wonder and amazement that can positively impact our emotional well-being.

In essence, the beauty of nature can uplift our spirits and fill us with a deep sense of joy and appreciation for the world around us from within.

Immersing oneself in nature is a therapeutic practice that can profoundly impact our mental and emotional well-being. By disconnecting from the distractions of modern life and embracing the present moment, we can cultivate a deeper connection with ourselves and those around us. This respite from the stresses and anxieties of daily life can lead to a sense of profound peace and contentment, allowing us to recharge and return to our daily routines with renewed energy and clarity.

Embarking to immerse oneself in nature can be a transformative experience. The sheer magnitude of the sky, with its endless expanse of clouds and shimmering stars, can evoke a sense of profound humility and insignificance. Similarly, being in the presence of the ocean, with its magnificent waves and powerful tides, can inspire feelings of awe and reverence.

And when standing before the grandeur of the mountains, with their towering peaks and rugged terrain, one cannot help but feel a deep sense of connection to the ancient forces of the earth. In these moments, we are reminded of our place in the vast universe and can feel a sense of connection to something greater than ourselves.

How to access bliss in nature:
An abundance of opportunities is available through nature to achieve a state of pure joy and contentment. Allow me to suggest a few options for you to consider:

1. If you're looking to escape the hustle and bustle of daily life and find some peace and quiet, one great option is to seek a tranquil natural setting. Whether it's a lush forest, a serene park, a peaceful beach, or even just the tranquil surroundings of your backyard, immersing yourself in the beauty of nature can be an excellent way to recharge your batteries and find a sense of solitude.
So go ahead and take a deep breath, let the world's worries slip away, and enjoy the peaceful serenity of the natural world around you.

2. Please take a moment to settle into a comfortable position, whether sitting or lying down. Once you've found your ideal one, gently close your eyes and take a deep breath in and out. Allow yourself to become fully immersed in the natural world, taking in all the sounds, smells, and sensations you can detect. Let these natural elements guide you into deep relaxation and tranquility.

To maintain a healthy and balanced state of mind, you must let go of any worries or concerns weighing you down. It is recommended that you take a few moments to relax and concentrate on the present moment, allowing yourself to fully unwind and let go of any negative thoughts or emotions holding you back. By taking this time to prioritize your mental well-being, you can approach each day with a clear and focused mindset.

Please take a moment to gently open your eyes and fully embrace the sheer magnificence of nature surrounding you. Take a few deep breaths and observe the vast array of colors, shapes, and textures in the natural world with awe and appreciation. From the vibrant hues of the flowers to the intricate patterns of the leaves, every aspect of nature is an actual work of art that deserves our admiration and respect. So take your time and allow yourself to be fully immersed in the beauty of character.

Allow yourself to bask in the sun's soothing warmth as it caresses your skin, the gentle breeze lightly tousling your hair, and the solid earth beneath your feet, grounding you in the present moment. Engage all of your senses and become fully present in the breathtaking beauty of nature and discover yourself from within. You will experience a feeling of inner bliss.

Conclusively, if you're feeling overwhelmed, stressed, or anxious, taking a break and spending time in nature can provide a deep sense of peace and tranquility. This simple yet powerful approach offers numerous benefits to your overall well-being. Scientific studies have shown that spending time in nature can improve the quality of your sleep, enhance cognitive function, boost your immune system, decrease inflammation, promote social bonding, and stimulate creativity.

So, step outside next time you feel stressed and connect with the natural world. You'll be amazed at how much it can improve your physical, mental, and emotional health from within.

Chapter 5: Doing Something You Love

Participating in activities you genuinely enjoy is imperative as they have numerous benefits. Firstly, engaging in such activities can aid in relaxation and help alleviate stress. By focusing on something that brings you joy, you can stay more present and let go of any anxieties and worries plaguing your mind. This, in turn, can significantly reduce stress and anxiety levels, resulting in an overall improvement in mental well-being.

Partaking in activities that bring you joy and fulfillment contributes to your well-being. Investing your time and energy into pursuing your passions can help you find a greater sense of purpose and meaning in your life. Whether it's a hobby, sport, or creative outlet, participating in enjoyable activities can offer a necessary break from the pressures of daily life and enhance feelings of contentment and satisfaction.

So, take the time to explore your interests and incorporate them into your routine. You will likely find that the benefits of pursuing your passions extend beyond just the activity itself.

Engaging in activities that bring you joy can be entertaining. And cultivate relationships with those with similar interests. This, in turn, can foster stronger social bonds, leading to a more gratifying and wholesome life experience. By engaging in activities that align with your passions, you could connect with individuals with similar values and perspectives, leading to a sense of belonging and community.

The social connections formed through shared interests also provide opportunities for personal growth and development as you learn from others and expand your knowledge and skills. Ultimately, prioritizing activities that bring you joy may enhance your mental and emotional well-being and enrich your social life and overall quality of life.

Why is doing something you love essential?

- Many of us find great happiness in pursuing hobbies and interests such as traveling, playing sports, reading, hiking, dancing, reading, spending quality time with loved ones, and volunteering in orphanages, domestic violence shelters, or old age homes. These activities offer a sense of meaning and fulfillment in our lives. However, have you ever considered taking your passion to the next level and turning it into a career?

  Imagine being able to earn a living doing what you love most. It can be an enriching experience and provide a sense of purpose that few other career paths can match.

- It's common for individuals to feel that pursuing their dream career is out of reach. However, it's important to remember that achieving this goal is possible with dedication and perseverance. While there may be roadblocks along the way, the sense of fulfillment and joy that comes from following one's passion is immeasurable.

  Despite the challenges that may arise, pursuing what truly makes you happy regarding your career path is vital. By doing so, you'll find professional success and personal fulfillment in your daily life.

- Participating in activities that ignite your passions is a fundamental element that offers numerous benefits. To begin with, engaging in such activities brings immense joy and fulfillment. By investing your time and energy into something you truly love, your productivity and motivation levels are bound to soar. Furthermore, pursuing your passions stimulates your creativity and innovation skills, positively impacting various aspects of your life. Ultimately, prioritizing your desires leads to more content and satisfying life.

- Participating in activities that genuinely resonate with your passions and values can provide an incredible purpose and fulfillment. Engaging in work that deeply resonates with your soul can positively impact the world and contribute to the greater good. This sense of purpose and satisfaction is unmatched and can be a powerful motivator to continue pursuing your passions.

  Additionally, following your passion can help you form authentic connections with like-minded individuals who share your interests and values. This can lead to substantial and meaningful relationships, as you are more likely to meet people who truly understand and support you.

- Discovering a career that genuinely aligns with your unique passions and interests can indeed feel like a challenging journey. However, it is a journey that is undoubtedly worth taking, as the rewards of finding your true calling are immeasurable. Turning your passion into a viable career may require both patience and persistence. There may be moments when you feel disheartened or uninspired but it is essential to keep pushing forward.
If you possess a genuine passion for something, you undoubtedly have the power to overcome any obstacle in your way. Pursuing your passion is vital to leading a happier and more fulfilling life as it can fundamentally change your perspective and imbue your daily life with a profound sense of purpose and meaning.

Benefits of doing something you love for accessing bliss

- There are numerous advantages to pursuing your passion. Engaging in activities that genuinely interest you can provide a sense of fulfillment and purpose. It can also lead to increased creativity, motivation, and productivity. Pursuing your passion can also enhance your well-being by reducing stress and improving your mental and emotional health. Therefore, it is essential to carve out time to pursue your interests and follow your heart.

- **Increased happiness and well-being:**
Participating in enjoyable activities that align with your passions has positively impacted your emotional well-being. When you engage in activities that you are passionate about, you are tapping into your innate talents and abilities in a way that provides a sense of fulfillment and satisfaction. As a result, you may experience heightened levels of happiness and satisfaction in your daily life.

  So, it is worthwhile to prioritize activities that bring you joy and align with your passions as they can significantly impact your overall happiness and well-being.

- **Improved productivity and creativity:**
When an individual possesses an intense enthusiasm for a particular interest or activity, they tend to experience heightened engagement and motivation, leading to increased productivity and enhanced creativity. This phenomenon can be observed across various domains and has significantly impacted an individual's overall satisfaction and well-being. Therefore, it is crucial to identify and nurture one's passions to achieve optimal fulfillment and success.

- **A stronger sense of purpose:**
Participating in activities that align with your interests and ignite passion can significantly enhance your overall sense of fulfillment and well-being. Engaging in genuinely enjoyable activities can provide a deep understanding of purpose and meaning, which can be

incredibly rewarding. This feeling of purpose can be further amplified when your actions positively impact those around you, contributing to greater happiness and fulfillment.

- **Deeper connections with others:**
  When you experience a profound fascination with a particular topic or pursuit, you are inclined to form stronger connections with individuals who possess similar interests. These relationships can develop into meaningful and rewarding friendships and partnerships that contribute to your inner well-being.

- **A more fulfilling life:**
  Participating in activities that you find enjoyable and fulfilling can significantly impact your overall well-being, boosting your sense of happiness, contentment, and satisfaction in life. This is because when you engage in things that align with your true self and values, you feel a greater sense of purpose and meaning.

  Doing what you love and enjoy makes you more likely to experience positive emotions and a greater understanding of fulfillment, ultimately leading to a more fulfilling and rewarding life from within.

If you are not pursuing your passion at the moment, there are ways you can work toward realizing it.

- **Start by identifying your passions:**
  Know more about your diverse talents and interests. What sets you apart, and what special abilities do you possess? Additionally, what hobbies or passions do

you enjoy indulging in? Lastly, what activities bring you the most happiness and fulfillment?

- **Do some research on different career paths and opportunities:**
  Many resources are available to you both online and at your local library. Whether you need academic sources for a research project or looking for leisure reading material, numerous options are available to meet your specific requirements. These resources may include digital databases, e-books, physical books, academic journals, magazines, and newspapers. By taking advantage of these resources, you can expand your knowledge and stay informed on various topics.

- **Don't be afraid to take risks:**
  If you happen upon an opportunity to pursue a passion that ignites joy within you, it's crucial to seize it without hesitation. The possibilities that arise from such a decision are endless and could ultimately lead you on a fulfilling and rewarding journey.

- **Be persistent:**
  Finding a way to make a living from doing what you truly love can be challenging and require patience and perseverance. However, staying focused and committed to your dream is essential if you have a genuine passion for something. With determination and hard work, you will eventually figure out how to turn your power into a successful career. Remember, the key is to never give up on your dreams and keep pushing forward, no matter how difficult the journey may seem.

It's essential to keep in mind that pursuing your passions isn't just about achieving perfection or reaching lofty goals. Instead, it's about finding something that brings you joy and a sense of fulfillment. So, feel free to try new things and explore different avenues. What matters is that you continue to move forward and actively work toward your aspirations, big or small. Always remember that persistence and a willingness to strive toward your dreams are the keys to success.

Upon finishing this chapter, you may have gained a new understanding of the importance of pursuing your passions. If you are drawn to a particular area of interest, please carefully contemplate all the potential paths. Doing so may reveal unexpected opportunities and avenues for personal growth that you had not previously considered. Remember, following your heart can lead to some of the most rewarding experiences of your life.

Different activities that people love to do

People participate in many activities that bring them joy and relaxation in their leisure time. These activities range from indulging in a hobby to spending quality time with loved ones. Some of the most popular activities that individuals engage in during their free time include reading, exercising, traveling, watching movies, playing sports, and exploring new interests. The possibilities are endless, and the choice of activity ultimately depends on personal preference and individual circumstances.

- **Reading:**

  For many people, reading books is a cherished pastime that offers a welcome respite from the stresses of everyday life. Beyond providing a source of relaxation, books can also be a valuable tool for expanding one's horizons and developing new perspectives.

  Whether delving into a classic novel or exploring the latest non-fiction bestseller, there is no shortage of opportunities to learn and grow through the power of literature.

- **Watching movies or TV:**

  Indulging in watching movies or TV can be a delightful and engaging activity, providing an escape from the humdrum of daily life. Moreover, it can be a fantastic means of strengthening relationships and fostering deep connections with those we hold dear.

- **Listening to music:**

  For most individuals, indulging in music is a highly effective means of unwinding and alleviating stress. Moreover, it is an excellent source of inspiration and motivation, reinvigorating one's spirit. It's widely acknowledged that music is a universally cherished art form.

- **Playing sports or games:**

  Participating in physical activities such as sports or games helps keep one's body in shape and provides an enjoyable experience. Moreover, it presents an excellent opportunity to interact with new people and expand one's social circle. The benefits of engaging in such activities are not only limited to physical health but also contribute to mental well-being.

Therefore, incorporating sports or games into one's daily routine can work wonders in maintaining a healthy and happy lifestyle.

- **Going for walks or hikes:**

  Going for a leisurely stroll or embarking on a hiking adventure is a fantastic way to stay active and reconnect with the great outdoors. Not only does it provide a physical workout but it can also serve as a mental escape from the hustle and bustle of everyday life. Many individuals find solace in walking or hiking and reap the benefits of exercise and fresh air.

- **Spending time with friends or family:**

  There is nothing quite like spending quality time with the people you love. It is a beautiful way to connect deeper and create lasting memories you can cherish for years. Whether it's a simple night in or an adventurous outing, sharing experiences with loved ones is a fantastic way to bask in the joys of life and have a great time together.

- **Traveling:**

  Venturing out into various corners of the globe is a remarkable way to fully engage with diverse cultures and unearth unexplored terrains. Moreover, embarking on a journey can present an incredible opportunity for individual development and a more profound comprehension of our intricate world.

- **Learning new skills:**

  One of the most effective ways to challenge yourself and maintain mental stimulation is by broadening your skill set. Not only can this increase your opportunities for career advancement but it also allows you to delve into fresh areas of personal interest. You can keep your mind active, engaged, and open to new possibilities by continuously learning new things.

- **Volunteering:**
Contributing to improving your community and effecting positive change can be accomplished through volunteering your time and efforts. Not only does this allow you to connect with and engage new individuals but it also presents the possibility of learning and developing novel skills. By dedicating yourself to a cause or organization, you can make a substantial impact and leave a lasting impression on those around you.

- As a child who grew up without parental support, I developed a deep passion for mental health advocacy. Through volunteer work at childcare homes for victims of domestic violence and sexual abuse, I've made a meaningful impact. Providing a support system for these children is an honor I cherish, and it's gratifying to know that my efforts have positively influenced their lives.

  By contributing funds for their basic needs, such as toiletries, clothes, food, stationery, and education, I've helped create a better world for those who need it most. I've discovered a meaningful way to give back to the universe what I received as a child. Volunteering gave me immense pleasure from within.

These are just a few activities people love to do in their free time. The most important thing is to find activities that you enjoy and make you happy.

Here are some additional thoughts on different activities that people love to do:

- When it comes to choosing free-time activities, there are no correct or incorrect answers. Opting for activities that bring you joy and contentment is crucial.
- Engaging in activities that challenge you and aid your personal growth is equally important. This could entail acquiring new skills, exploring new destinations, or volunteering your time to assist others.
- Ultimately, setting aside time for activities you love is crucial, mainly when surrounded by those you care about. This could include spending time with family and friends, going on dates, or simply relaxing and conversing.
- *No matter what activities you choose in your free time, the most important thing is to enjoy yourself and make memories you will cherish for years.*

Why doing what you love is essential for inner bliss?

Experiencing happiness is truly a remarkable feeling. It is a state of contentment and well-being that brings about a sense of satisfaction and fulfillment. When we are happy, we feel joy in our hearts radiating throughout our entire being. However, a deeper level of happiness, known as inner bliss, stems from within. This type of happiness is a fleeting emotion and a feeling of peace, purpose, and interconnectedness.

It's a sense of being in tune with oneself and the world around us, which can bring a profound sense of happiness and contentment.

Several elements contribute to an individual's happiness, but one that stands out is doing what you love. Participating in activities that align with your unique strengths and talents creates a profound sense of purpose and fulfillment. Pursuing your passions and interests can also create flow and engagement, enhancing overall well-being. Ultimately, it is essential to prioritize following your passions and interests to achieve inner happiness.

Participating in activities that ignite your innermost passions and interests can significantly benefit you. Engaging in something that genuinely captivates your attention makes you feel more motivated, fulfilled, and purposeful. Additionally, pursuing your passions can lead to personal growth as you may gain new skills and knowledge while exploring your interests. Overall, engaging in activities that you are passionate about can bring more positivity and satisfaction into your life.

Developing healthy self-esteem and confidence can profoundly impact one's overall well-being. Individuals who feel secure in their abilities and worth are likelier to approach challenges with a positive attitude and determination. This can lead to increased productivity and creativity in various areas of life, such as work, relationships, and personal hobbies.

In addition to the practical benefits, having a solid sense of self can also help individuals find greater purpose and fulfillment in life. When confident in our values and aspirations, we are better equipped to pursue our goals and connect with others with similar interests. This can lead to meaningful relationships, and a sense of belonging that is essential for our emotional and mental health.

Ultimately, investing in our self-esteem and confidence is one of the most valuable things we can do for ourselves. Recognizing our worth and potential can unlock new opportunities and experiences that enrich our lives and bring us closer to our goals.

If you are not currently doing what you love, you can take steps to make it happen. First, take some time to think about what you are passionate about. What are your interests? What are your strengths and talents? Once you better understand what you love, you can explore ways to make it a part of your life.

To enhance your overall happiness and sense of inner peace, it's vital to focus your energy and time on activities that truly ignite your passion. Doing so will allow you to transform your life profoundly and meaningfully. It's important to understand that engaging in what you love is crucial when achieving true inner bliss. When you immerse yourself in activities that bring you joy and fulfillment, you'll naturally feel more content, fulfilled, and at peace with yourself and the world around you.

So if you're seeking a greater sense of happiness and tranquility, start by identifying the things that truly light you up and make them a priority in your life.

Participating in activities that bring you joy and satisfaction can positively impact your productivity and success. When you engage in things you genuinely enjoy, you are more likely to find the motivation and determination to persevere through difficult circumstances. This can ultimately lead to increased success and fulfillment in your personal and professional life. Therefore, making time for the activities that bring you the most joy is essential.

Exploring and pursuing your passions is a powerful way to uncover your life's purpose. By immersing yourself in activities you genuinely enjoy, you can tap into a deep sense of fulfillment and meaning that can be elusive through other avenues. Not only that but following your passions can also enable you to positively impact the world and feel like you're contributing to something meaningful.

Whether through creative expression, community service, or any other passion, dedicating time and energy to what you love can lead to a more fulfilling and purposeful life.

Engaging in activities you enjoy can help you connect with like-minded individuals who share your passions, fostering a sense of camaraderie and encouragement crucial for achieving personal contentment.

Ultimately, leading an authentic life that aligns with your innermost self entails wholeheartedly pursuing your passions. When you engage in activities that ignite your enthusiasm, you tap into an inherent sense of joy within you rather than seeking it out externally. By identifying and embracing your passions, you can cultivate a sense of fulfillment and live a genuinely satisfying life.

Commencing a journey toward your desired destination requires taking the initial step. Even if you're unsure of which path to pursue, it's essential to start exploring your interests and allow yourself to be guided by curiosity. By doing so, you may discover unexpected and exciting aspects of yourself. It's crucial to remember that pursuing your passion isn't solely about achieving perfection or grandeur.

It's about learning something that brings you genuine joy and fulfillment from within. Therefore, don't hesitate to experiment and try out new things. The most important thing is to keep moving forward and never abandon your aspirations.

Chapter 6: Gratitude

Expressing gratitude is a powerful emotion that can transform our lives significantly. It involves acknowledging and appreciating the good things in our lives, regardless of their size or significance. When we practice gratitude, we shift our focus from lacking to what we already have, leading to a sense of abundance and contentment.

The act of gratitude positively impacts our relationships, allowing us to form stronger connections and a sense of belonging. They are more likely to feel valued and supported by expressing appreciation for others, promoting mutual support and kindness.

In addition to promoting positive relationships, gratitude also positively impacts our mental well-being. Studies have shown that practicing gratitude can reduce stress, increase happiness, and improve overall life satisfaction. By focusing on the positive aspects of our lives, we can train our minds to see the good in all situations, leading to a more positive outlook.

Furthermore, gratitude promotes resilience in times of adversity. We are better equipped to overcome challenges and setbacks by maintaining a positive outlook and being grateful for what we have.

In conclusion, cultivating gratitude can profoundly affect our lives, enhancing our relationships, boosting our mental well-being, and increasing our resilience. It is important to take a moment each day to reflect on what we are grateful for and spread this powerful emotion to create a happier world for ourselves and others.

What is gratitude?

Expressing gratitude is a profound and meaningful act that involves acknowledging and appreciating the positive aspects of one's life. This powerful emotion has the potential to provide numerous benefits, including improved physical and mental health, stronger relationships, and an enhanced sense of overall well-being. By cultivating an attitude of gratitude, we can gain a greater appreciation for the blessings in our lives, no matter how small they may seem.

It's interesting to note that the term "gratitude" actually has its origins in the Latin word "gratia", which can be translated to mean "grace", "favor", or "kindness". It's a way that people can show appreciation for something that has been done for them, whether through words or actions. Some common examples of demonstrating gratitude might include saying "thank you", offering gifts, or performing acts of kindness to show how much you appreciate someone else's efforts.

Benefits of gratitude for accessing bliss

Practicing gratitude has been extensively researched and proven to yield numerous benefits. Studies have shown that expressing gratitude can have a significant positive impact on an individual's overall well-being. Such gifts can include improved mental health, lower stress levels, and a heightened sense of happiness and contentment. By consciously focusing on what we are thankful for, we can cultivate a more positive outlook on life and experience greater personal fulfillment.

Reduce stress and anxiety:

It's been said that when we take a moment to focus on the good things in our lives, it can have a significant impact on our mental well-being. By shifting our attention away from the stressors and worries that can weigh us down, we can reduce the stress and anxiety levels we experience. This can effectively manage our emotions and maintain a positive outlook, even in challenging times.

Ultimately, by practicing gratitude and focusing on the positive aspects of our lives, we can cultivate a sense of inner peace and contentment that can help us navigate life's ups and downs with greater ease and resilience.

Improve our mood:

Expressing gratitude can significantly enhance our well-being and happiness. When we actively acknowledge and appreciate the positive aspects of our lives, we can cultivate a more optimistic outlook and ultimately experience greater contentment. This simple yet powerful practice can help us stay grounded and focused on what truly matters, leading to a more fulfilling and satisfying life.

Strengthen our relationships:

When we take the time to express our gratitude toward others, it can positively impact our relationships. It communicates to others that we recognize and value their presence in our lives, creating a more profound sense of connection and appreciation. By showing gratitude, we benefit those around us and cultivate a more positive and fulfilling outlook.

Improve our physical health:

Research has proven that expressing gratitude can positively affect our physical well-being. It can aid in reducing inflammation, lowering blood pressure, and strengthening the immune system. There are several techniques to cultivate gratitude. Listed below are some suggestions:

Keep a gratitude journal:

Dedicating moments of your day to introspect and jot down three things you are grateful for is highly recommended. These can be as rudimentary as your physical well-being, the companionship of your dear ones, the comfort of your abode, or the security of your employment. Expressing appreciation can significantly improve your outlook toward life and attract more optimism into your existence.

Start each day with a gratitude ritual:

There are several ways in which an individual can practice gratitude. One commonly used method is reciting a prayer, where one expresses their thankfulness for the blessings in their life. Another approach is to take a moment to carefully contemplate the positive aspects of their life, such as family, friends, health, and other privileges. Additionally, some people prefer to jot down three things they are grateful for daily to cultivate a grateful mindset.

All these approaches can help one appreciate the good things in their life and foster a positive attitude toward their circumstances.

Do something kind for someone else:

One of the most beautiful ways to make a positive difference is by expressing gratitude toward others. It is a simple yet powerful gesture that can profoundly impact the recipient. By taking a moment to acknowledge and appreciate someone else's efforts or kindness, we not only make them feel valued and respected but also cultivate a culture of gratitude and compassion in society. So let us consciously express our gratitude toward others and spread positivity in the world.

Spend time in nature:

Devoting some time to immersing ourselves in the natural world can be a truly transformative experience, enabling us to forge a profound connection with the awe-inspiring environment that envelops us. Doing so makes us more attuned to the small yet wondrous elements that imbue our lives with joy and meaning.

Incorporating the practice of gratitude into our daily routine can be a transformative experience, yielding numerous benefits for our mental and physical well-being. By focusing on and expressing gratitude for the positive aspects of our lives, we can reduce stress and anxiety, uplift our mood, and strengthen our relationships with others. Additionally, research suggests that gratitude is linked to improved immune function, better sleep quality, and even reduced symptoms of depression.

Thus, consider making gratitude a regular part of your routine to enhance your overall quality of life.

Experiencing tough times can be a daunting challenge but it's important to remember that being grateful isn't about striving for perfection. Rather, it's about acknowledging and embracing the positive aspects of your life, no matter how small they may be. It's about taking the time to appreciate what you have instead of constantly comparing yourself to others. Gratitude is neither a burden nor a way to feel guilty about what you don't have. It's a way of acknowledging and being thankful for the blessings you do have, even if they don't meet all of your desires.

One of the most critical aspects of cultivating a grateful heart is discovering what methods work best for you and committing to a consistent practice. By dedicating your time and effort to this pursuit, you can create a habit of gratitude that will ultimately lead to greater joy and happiness. Whether through daily journaling, meditation, or other mindful practices, the key is to find what resonates with you and make it a part of your daily routine.

With patience, perseverance, and a willingness to learn, you can develop a habit of gratitude that will bring lasting benefits to your life.

How to keep a gratitude journal?

Expressing gratitude is a powerful and transformative emotion that has numerous benefits for our mental and physical well-being. It uplifts our mood, promotes positivity, and strengthens our bond with others. Additionally, it helps us to cope with stress, anxiety, and depression effectively, making it an essential practice in our daily lives.

One of the best ways to cultivate gratitude is by keeping a gratitude journal. This simple practice involves writing down things we are thankful for daily. By doing so, we can develop a positive mindset and focus on the good things in our lives. We can use a conventional journal to record our thoughts or get creative and use a more artistic medium, such as a photo album or collage, to capture our gratitude. Regardless of the medium, regularly expressing gratitude is a powerful tool for improving our well-being.

You can use various methods if you're interested in starting a gratitude journal. To help you begin your journey toward a more grateful mindset, we've compiled a few tips and tricks that you may find useful. By following these guidelines, you'll be well on your way to cultivating a more positive outlook.

Choose a time and place that works for you:

Some people like to journal in the morning, while others prefer to do it at night. You can also journal during your lunch break or any other time of day that works for you. Find a time and place where you won't be interrupted and where you can relax and focus on your thoughts.

Start small:

If you are just starting out with journaling, it can be helpful to begin by writing down three things you are grateful for each day. This can be a great way to cultivate a positive mindset and focus on the good things in life. As you become more comfortable with the practice, you should gradually increase the number of things you reflect on. This can help you become more mindful and present daily, providing a valuable record of your thoughts and experiences.

So if you want to start a journaling practice, why not try this simple technique? It may be the perfect way to begin your journey toward greater self-awareness and personal growth.

Be specific:

Rather than giving a general statement like "I appreciate my family", it would be more effective to provide a specific example of something they did that made you feel grateful. One way of doing this is by expressing appreciation toward your mother for taking the time and effort to prepare a delicious dinner for you tonight. This way, you acknowledge her hard work and show gratitude toward her for improving your day.

Be present:

When composing entries in your journal, it is of utmost importance to focus on the present moment and acknowledge the abundance of blessings in your life. Refraining from lingering on past events or fretting over future uncertainties is advisable. By remaining in the present and expressing gratitude for your life's positive aspects, you can cultivate a sense of peace and contentment that will enhance your overall well-being.

Get creative:

Maintaining a gratitude journal is personal; no one-size-fits-all approach can be deemed correct or incorrect. One may express appreciation through the traditional pen and paper or opt for a more creative outlet such as art, photography, or music to convey gratitude. It is entirely up to the individual to determine the most effective method for capturing and acknowledging the blessings in their life.

Don't give up:

Keeping a gratitude journal is a task that demands commitment and endurance. It is a practice that requires consistent effort and patience to see its positive impact on one's life. It may take some time to notice the benefits but persisting and remaining dedicated to the task is important. Consistent writing down what you are grateful for can help shift your mindset and focus on the positive aspects of your life.

Over time, you may notice improvements in your overall well-being and outlook. So, keep at it and trust that the benefits of gratitude will eventually become evident.

I want to offer some additional guidance regarding the upkeep of a gratitude journal. Take the time to reflect on what you are grateful for each day, and jot them down in the journal. Additionally, it can be helpful to write about why you are thankful for each item on your list, as this can deepen your appreciation and understanding of the positive aspects of your life.

Finally, make it a habit to consistently write in your gratitude journal, even if it's just a few sentences a day. This will help to reinforce the practice of gratitude and make it a regular part of your routine.

Use prompts:

If you're experiencing difficulty in expressing gratitude, using prompts can be an effective strategy to help get your thoughts flowing. A plethora of gratitude prompts are readily available online or in books and can serve as a helpful tool in guiding you toward a more thankful mindset.

Share your journal with others:

Sharing your personal diary with close friends or family members effectively establishes stronger connections with them. It provides a platform for open communication, allowing you to share your thoughts, feelings, and experiences with others in a safe and supportive environment. This can help you feel more understood, validated, and cared for. However, before sharing your diary, you must ensure you are comfortable with the idea and trust the person you share it with.

Make it a habit:

As you continue to write in your journal, the process becomes more comfortable and second nature. It is recommended that you make journaling a regular habit, whether writing every day or every few days. This practice can have many benefits for your mental and emotional well-being, as well as provide a valuable record of your life experiences and personal growth.

Maintaining a gratitude journal has positively affected one's mental health and overall well-being. By taking the time to regularly reflect on the things we are grateful for, we can cultivate a sense of appreciation and positivity in our lives. Additionally, a gratitude journal can help reduce stress and anxiety, improve sleep quality, and enhance our relationships with others. Incorporating this simple practice into our daily routine can significantly impact our happiness and satisfaction with life.

Research has demonstrated that it is highly beneficial to maintain a gratitude journal regularly. Those who engage in this practice have been found to enjoy increased happiness levels and report a greater sense of overall well-being than those who do not. By focusing on the positive aspects of our lives, gratitude can also effectively reduce stress and anxiety levels.

Moreover, studies have shown that practicing gratitude can improve sleep quality by reducing negative thoughts and worries that might otherwise keep us awake. This positive habit can also foster increased optimism and positivity in our outlook on life as we learn to cultivate a greater appreciation for the good things in our lives. Ultimately, gratitude can also help us to develop stronger, more meaningful relationships by encouraging us to be more mindful of our loved ones and to express our appreciation for them regularly.

Establishing a gratitude journal can be a highly beneficial practice that can significantly improve your overall well-being. This simple yet effective approach requires you to focus on the positive aspects of your life and express gratitude toward the things that you possess. Doing so can enhance your mental and physical health while cultivating a positive mindset to help you navigate life's challenges more easily.

If you haven't yet, give gratitude practice a try. It can positively impact your overall well-being by increasing happiness, reducing stress, and improving relationships.

Maintaining a gratitude journal is one simple yet impactful method for improving one's mental and physical well-being. This powerful tool has the potential to elevate our mood, increase positivity, and foster stronger social connections. Moreover, it can alleviate feelings of stress, anxiety, and depression, making it an invaluable practice for those seeking to enhance the quality of their lives.

By reflecting on the things we are grateful for, we can cultivate a sense of appreciation and contentment that can positively impact every aspect of our lives. Whether it be the people in our lives, our health, or even the simple pleasures we enjoy, a gratitude journal can help us recognize and celebrate the abundance surrounding us and within us.

Chapter 7: Forgiveness

Why is forgiveness important?

Forgiveness is a powerful tool that can help you liberate yourself from the detrimental effects of negative emotions. When you forgive someone, it doesn't mean that you're condoning or disregarding their wrongdoing. Instead, it's a way to release yourself from anger, bitterness, and resentment that their actions may have caused you. Forgiveness is a process that enables you to let go of those emotions and move forward with your life.

It's a way to restore your inner peace and well-being and reclaim your power and control over your feelings and emotions. So, if you're struggling with negative emotions toward someone, consider forgiving them for healing yourself and finding inner peace.

Forgiveness is a powerful and transformative action that deeply and meaningfully impacts our lives. When we choose to forgive, we can let go of the heavy burden of negative emotions that can weigh us down and hold us back. By releasing ourselves from these negative feelings, we create space for healing and growth, allowing us to move forward with renewed energy and focus.

Whether we are forgiving others or ourselves, forgiveness is essential to our personal and spiritual journeys, helping us become more compassionate, understanding, and loving human beings. So let us embrace forgiveness as a vital tool for self-improvement and healing, and let us all move forward together toward a brighter and more positive future.

There are several advantages to practicing forgiveness. It can assist us in various ways, such as enabling us to rewrite the narrative of a negative experience and move forward in a positive direction. Additionally, forgiveness can bring about inner peace and tranquility, and promote healthier relationships and interactions with others. It is truly a powerful tool that can have a significant impact on our overall well-being.

1. It is crucial to prioritize our mental health by effectively managing stress and anxiety. One effective method of doing so is by practicing forgiveness. When we hold onto feelings of anger and resentment toward others, it can lead to heightened levels of stress and anxiety that can negatively impact our well-being.

   However, forgiving those who have wronged us can release us from these negative emotions and allow us to experience greater relaxation and inner peace. We can cultivate a more positive and healthier mindset by focusing on forgiveness.

2. It's worth noting that taking the initiative to forgive others can have many benefits for our physical well-being. Extensive research has found that forgiveness is directly linked to reductions in blood pressure and

heart rate, indicating that it can be a powerful tool for maintaining a healthy body.

3. Nurturing and solidifying our relationships with others is essential to leading a fulfilling life. A crucial component of maintaining these connections is forgiveness. By forgiving those who have wronged us, we can begin to mend damaged relationships and cultivate deeper, more meaningful bonds with the people we hold dear. Through this process, we can strengthen our connections with others and enhance our sense of well-being and happiness.

4. Forgiveness holds the key to unlocking our inner happiness and well-being. Letting go of past grievances brings a sense of relief and enables us to experience a greater understanding of contentment and freedom. Through forgiveness, we can break free from negativity and embrace new opportunities and beginnings with a more positive outlook. By forgiving, we open ourselves to a world of endless possibilities and pave the way for a brighter tomorrow.

Forgiveness can be arduous, particularly when we harbor anger and bitterness toward someone who has caused us pain. However, it is important to recognize that the benefits of forgiveness are significant and can positively impact our emotional and mental well-being. By letting go of negative emotions and choosing to forgive, we free ourselves from holding onto grudges and allow ourselves to move forward healthily and productively.

Forgiveness is a powerful tool that can help us cultivate stronger, more fulfilling relationships with others and ourselves.

If you're struggling to forgive someone, it's important to understand that forgiveness is a process that takes time and effort to let go of negative emotions. It's not a one-time event that happens overnight. Seeking the help of a therapist or counselor can be beneficial in understanding your feelings and finding ways to cope with them. It may also be helpful to establish a connection with the person you're trying to forgive, whether through conversation, writing a letter, or simply practicing empathy toward them.

By taking these steps, you can work toward releasing any lingering resentment and finding peace within yourself.

Forgiveness is not as simple as saying, "I forgive you". It is a journey that requires patience and effort. It is about letting go of negative feelings and moving forward. This process involves examining the hurt caused, understanding the emotions involved, and consciously forgiving. It may take time and effort but the benefits of forgiveness are worth it. By embracing this process, one can experience powerful healing and transformation, both emotionally and spiritually.

Forgiveness is not just about the other person; it is also about releasing oneself from anger and resentment. It is about finding peace within oneself and moving forward with a renewed sense of purpose.

Here are some additional tips for forgiving someone:

1. Recognizing and accepting your emotions, even those that might be uncomfortable, such as anger, resentment, or hurt, is essential to emotional well-being. It's

important not to suppress or deny these emotions, as they can build up and cause further harm. Acknowledging and processing your feelings can help you better understand yourself and your needs, leading to greater inner peace and balance.

2. When interacting with another person, it's crucial to consider their perspective. Although you may not agree with their choices or behavior, taking the time to comprehend their reasoning can offer valuable insights into their mindset and motivations. By doing so, you can better understand their origin and establish a more constructive and empathetic relationship with them.

3. Making the decision to forgive can be a truly transformative experience. Even though it's important to remember the events that led to the need for forgiveness, it's equally crucial to release any negative emotions you may have been holding onto. Doing so allows you to free yourself from negative feelings and move forward with renewed peace and positivity.

4. Forgiveness is a process that requires patience and dedication. It takes time and effort to achieve it. One way to start the journey toward forgiveness is by taking small steps. You could begin by thinking about the person compassionately, acknowledging that they are human and make mistakes like everyone else.
Another helpful step is to pray for them, wishing them well and sending positive energy their way. These small actions can go a long way toward healing and ultimately lead to forgiveness.

5. In the pursuit of forgiveness, it's crucial to maintain patience with oneself and remember that it's a process that takes time. It's natural to experience moments of feeling like progress has regressed. However, what's essential is to keep forging ahead despite the obstacles that present themselves along the way.

Forgiving is a gift we can give ourselves as it allows us to release any negative emotions holding us back. However, we understand that forgiving can sometimes be a challenging process. But it's important to know you are not alone in your struggle. There are numerous resources and tools available that can help you on your journey toward forgiveness. By committing to this process and persevering through the challenges, you can ultimately find the inner peace and freedom that comes with forgiving others.

Learning to forgive someone who has wronged us can be a challenging and emotionally complex journey. Forgiveness can profoundly impact our lives, not only by releasing us from negative emotions but also by fostering greater empathy and compassion. However, it's important to acknowledge that forgiveness is not a simple task, and it may require patience, dedication, and support from others.

Fortunately, many resources are available to assist individuals in their journey toward forgiveness, including therapy, support groups, and self-help books. By working through our feelings and cultivating forgiveness, we can attain greater inner peace and emotional well-being.

How to forgive someone

Forgiveness is a powerful tool that can have a transformative effect on our emotional and mental well-being. By releasing ourselves from negative emotions such as anger, resentment, and bitterness, we can open ourselves up to the possibility of healing and reconciliation. Nevertheless, forgiveness is no easy feat. It requires us to relinquish our desire for justice, which can be challenging and time-consuming.

Nonetheless, the rewards of forgiveness are immeasurable and the path to achieving it is well worth the effort.

If you are struggling to forgive someone, here are some steps you can take:

- Recognize your emotions. The initial step toward forgiveness is to acknowledge the pain and anger you are experiencing. Avoid suppressing your feelings or denying that you are hurt. Rather, permit yourself to feel your emotions and take time to mourn the end of your connection with the individual who caused you harm.

- Once you have acknowledged your emotions regarding a situation in which someone has wronged you, it can be helpful to take a step back and consider the motivations behind your actions. By empathizing with their thoughts and emotions at the time of the incident, you may better understand their perspective. This understanding can lead to a more compassionate view of the person who wronged you, which can ultimately aid in the process of forgiveness and moving forward. It's important to note that this does not excuse their behavior but provides a more nuanced understanding of the situation.

- When you're dealing with hurt and pain caused by someone, it's crucial to understand that forgiveness is a conscious decision. You're not obligated to do it but choosing to forgive can be incredibly liberating. Ignoring the person who wronged you takes a powerful step toward healing and moving on with your life.

  While it may not be easy, it's worth considering if you want to live a happier and more peaceful life. Remember, forgiveness is a choice only you can make, and it can profoundly impact your mental and emotional well-being.

- To achieve true forgiveness, releasing your desire for justice is crucial. This does not mean you must forget about the situation or condone the other person's actions. Rather, it means you are willing to relinquish your need for retribution and forgive the other person for any wrongdoings they may have committed against you.

  By doing so, you are absolving them of any debt you may hold against them and freeing yourself from resentment and anger. Forgiveness is a powerful tool that allows you to move forward and find peace within yourself.

- It is a fact of life that everyone experiences mistakes and painful situations at some point in their existence. If you are currently grappling with the challenge of forgiving someone who has caused you harm, it may be helpful to begin by extending forgiveness to yourself for any suffering you have endured. It is essential to recognize that self-forgiveness is a potent tool for healing and moving forward.

Adopt a compassionate attitude toward yourself and remember that you are not the only one who has to deal with such struggles. Doing so allows you to navigate the healing process more easily and gracefully.

- Should you find yourself struggling to forgive someone who has wronged you, consider seeking the assistance of a qualified professional. Whether it be a therapist or another type of counselor, these individuals can provide the tools and guidance necessary to process your emotions and develop a plan for forgiveness. Remember, forgiveness is a journey that takes time and effort.

  It's natural to experience setbacks along the way but by remaining committed to the process, you can ultimately let go of the pain and move forward with your life. Don't hesitate to seek help if needed; there's no shame in improving your emotional well-being.

If you're looking for additional ideas on forgiving someone, I can offer a few suggestions. One approach could be to try and see the situation from the other person's perspective, which may help you understand their motivations and actions. Another idea could be to communicate openly and honestly with the person and express how their actions have impacted you.

It may also be helpful to practice self-compassion and acknowledge that forgiveness is a process that takes time and effort. Finding forgiveness is a personal journey and may require different strategies for different situations.

- To effectively manage the stress that often accompanies the act of forgiveness, it is essential to prioritize self-care. One of the most important aspects of self-care is maintaining a healthy and balanced diet that provides your body with all the necessary nutrients to function optimally. Additionally, it is crucial to ensure you are getting enough restful sleep each night as this will help restore your energy levels and promote a sense of calm and relaxation.
Regular exercise is also a key component of self-care, as it supports your physical health and promotes emotional well-being by reducing stress and releasing endorphins that boost your mood. By prioritizing self-care, you can better manage the stress of forgiveness and maintain a healthy and balanced lifestyle.

- A supportive network of people around you is crucial for maintaining your emotional well-being. This can include trusted friends, family members, or even a licensed therapist. Engaging in open and honest conversations with someone you trust can help alleviate feelings of isolation and motivate you to pursue forgiveness. Forgiveness is a journey that can sometimes feel overwhelming but having a strong support system can make all the difference.

- When you're feeling down, it's essential to practice self-compassion. Treating yourself with kindness and respect is a powerful way to remind yourself of your worth. There are many ways to practice self-care, such as indulging in a soothing bubble bath, immersing yourself in a good book, or taking a refreshing walk in nature. Whatever method you choose, remember that you deserve to prioritize your well-being and cultivate deep self-love.

It's important to remember that forgiveness is not an instantaneous process but requires patience and effort. It's natural to feel frustrated or discouraged if you don't forgive someone immediately, but it's important to keep working. Give yourself the time and space you need to heal but also be proactive in taking steps toward forgiveness. With time and dedication, you will eventually reach your goal of forgiveness.

Offering forgiveness is a precious gift that you give to yourself. It allows you to release the pain and anguish of past experiences and provides a pathway to a more optimistic future. If you find it challenging to forgive someone, don't despair. Keep working on it; you will attain the peace and tranquility you desire with time. Remember that forgiveness is a process and it takes time to achieve. Nonetheless, by persisting in your efforts, you will ultimately reap the rewards of a more fulfilled and satisfying life.

The benefits of forgiveness in accessing bliss

The act of forgiveness holds great significance in our lives, as it can have a profound impact on our emotional and mental well-being. Forgiveness can liberate us from negative emotions such as anger, resentment, and bitterness and help us experience healing and reconciliation. However, it is not always an easy task to forgive someone. It requires significant effort, time, and patience as we must learn to relinquish our desire for justice and move forward with love and compassion.

Nonetheless, the benefits of forgiveness are immeasurable, and it can help us live a more fulfilling and peaceful life.

However, the benefits of forgiveness are well worth the effort. Forgiveness can lead to several positive outcomes, including:

- Studies have shown that incorporating forgiveness into one's life can positively impact mental and physical health. Specifically, individuals who practice forgiveness may experience reduced levels of stress, anxiety, and depression. In addition, forgiveness has been linked to improved sleep quality and a strengthened immune system. These findings suggest that forgiveness could be valuable for promoting overall well-being.

- Research has shown that forgiveness can profoundly impact our overall happiness and well-being. When we choose to forgive others, we release the negative emotions that can hold us back and create space for positive emotions like joy and peace to flourish. In other words, forgiveness is a compassionate act toward others and a powerful tool for personal growth and emotional healing. By embracing forgiveness, we can move past our pain and open ourselves up to a more fulfilling life.

- Forgiveness is a powerful and highly effective tool that can help repair relationships damaged by hurt or betrayal. When we choose to forgive someone, we demonstrate to them that we are willing to let go of the past and move forward positively and constructively. This can profoundly impact the nature of the relationship, leading to a deeper and more meaningful connection between the individuals involved.

Ultimately, forgiveness can be a transformative experience, allowing both parties to grow and evolve in ways that might not have been possible otherwise.

- In our journey toward spiritual enlightenment, forgiveness can play a pivotal role. By forgiving, we consciously prioritize love and understanding over anger and bitterness. This shift in mindset not only helps us find inner peace but also allows us to connect with our inner divinity. When we forgive, we let go of grudges and negative emotions, allowing for positive feelings such as compassion and empathy.

  This, in turn, leads to a heightened sense of spiritual awareness, allowing us to experience more profound levels of well-being and fulfillment.

In addition to these benefits, forgiveness can lead to a more general sense of bliss. Bliss is a state of perfect happiness and contentment. It is a feeling of peace with us and the world around us. Forgiveness can help us achieve this bliss by releasing us from the negative emotions holding us back. When we forgive, we free ourselves to experience the joy, love, and peace that are our birthright.

Of course, forgiveness is not always easy. It can be a challenging process and it takes time and effort. However, the rewards of forgiveness are well worth the effort. If you struggle to forgive someone, know you are not alone. There are many resources available to help you on your journey.

With time and effort, you can learn to forgive and experience the bliss that is your birthright.

Here are some specific examples of how forgiveness can lead to bliss:

- A woman abused by her father could forgive him after years of therapy. She realized that her father was also a victim of abuse and that he was acting out of his own pain. When she forgave him, she could let go of the anger and resentment she had been carrying around for so long. She also experienced a sense of peace and freedom that she had never known before.

- Forgiveness is a complex and lengthy process for a man betrayed by his wife. It takes time for him to accept that his trust has been broken and his heart has been wounded. However, he eventually realizes that holding onto anger and bitterness is not the way to live the rest of his life. By forgiving his wife, he can let go of the pain and move forward with peace and freedom. With time, he can find happiness again and focus on building a new life.

- Following a devastating event that completely shattered their family, they gradually came to appreciate the significance of forgiveness and the value of restoring relationships. They recognized that holding onto bitterness and animosity only led to further heartache and strife. Therefore, by opting to overlook their disagreements and prioritize their bond, they were able to mend their wounds and progress toward a brighter future.

Forgiveness is a powerful tool that can bring immense joy and contentment to our lives; countless examples demonstrate this. However, forgiving someone is not always easy, especially if they deeply hurt us. The good news is that many resources are available to help us on our journey toward forgiveness. Whether it's seeking guidance from a trusted friend or therapist, practicing self-reflection and empathy, or engaging in forgiveness exercises, there are many strategies we can use to cultivate forgiveness in our lives.

Of course, forgiveness is a process that requires dedication and patience but with time and effort, we can learn to let go of our anger and resentment and experience the happiness and peace that we truly deserve.

Forgiveness is a significant act that can profoundly impact our lives. It can enhance our mental and physical health, increase happiness and well-being, deepen relationships, and elevate our spiritual awareness. Furthermore, forgiveness can help us achieve bliss, perfect happiness, and contentment. If you find it challenging to forgive someone, remember that you are not alone. There are numerous resources available to assist you on your journey. With time and effort, you can learn to forgive and experience the bliss you are entitled to.

Chapter 8: Affirmations

What is an affirmation?

Affirmations are powerful tools that can transform one's thoughts and beliefs positively. By repeating positive statements to oneself, individuals can boost their self-esteem, work toward achieving their goals, and bring their desires into reality. These positive affirmations can help individuals reprogram their subconscious mind, allowing them to overcome negative thought patterns and limiting beliefs. With consistent practice, affirmations can help individuals cultivate a more positive mindset and manifest positive life changes.

The power and efficacy of affirmations lie in their ability to tap into the subconscious mind, which acts as a sponge, absorbing and retaining all our thoughts, beliefs, and experiences throughout our lives. By repeatedly affirming and reaffirming our commitment to a particular idea or goal, we effectively program our subconscious to adopt and internalize these new beliefs. Over time, this process can lead to a significant shift in our mindset and behavior, ultimately helping us achieve our desired success and fulfillment.

When you consistently repeat a positive statement, your subconscious mind gradually accepts it as truth and eventually manifests it in your physical reality. This means that by regularly affirming your confidence, you instill a sense of assurance in your daily activities and interactions with others. By acknowledging and embracing your self-worth through positive affirmations, you can improve your overall mindset and succeed tremendously in all aspects of your life.

How to create affirmations:

When creating affirmations, it is crucial to remember a few essential aspects. Firstly, it is important to formulate them positively, focusing on what you want to achieve rather than what you want to avoid. Make them specific and personal, tailored to your unique goals and aspirations. Lastly, use present tense language to reinforce the belief that these affirmations are already accurate and achievable. Following these guidelines can create powerful affirmations to help you reach your desired outcomes.

When crafting affirmations, it's critical to prioritize positive statements that emphasize the end goal rather than what you hope to avoid. By way of example, rather than saying, "I'm not scared to address a crowd", you could reframe this to "I exude confidence and eloquence when delivering public speeches". This methodology promotes a proactive and optimistic mindset, which can be instrumental in achieving success.

To maximize the effectiveness of using affirmations, it is recommended to keep them brief and straightforward. Doing so allows you to easily commit them to memory and increase the likelihood of regularly reciting them. This approach will help ensure that your affirmations become a habit and ultimately lead to positive changes in your thoughts and behaviors.

When repeating affirmations, using the present tense is crucial. This technique is beneficial because it helps create a belief that the statement is already true. For example, instead of saying, "I will be successful", it's better to say, "I am successful" to instill confidence and self-assurance. By using the present tense, you affirm that you already possess the qualities or capabilities needed for success rather than hoping for them in the future. This simple shift in language can make a significant impact on your mindset and overall success.

Incorporating regularly repeating affirmations into your daily routine is highly recommended. The more frequently you repeat them, the more deeply ingrained they become in your subconscious. Aiming for at least one repetition per day is advisable but repeating them multiple times throughout the day can significantly enhance their effectiveness. Consistency and dedication are vital in solidifying the positive impact of your affirmations on your overall well-being.

Benefits of affirmations:

Incorporating affirmations into one's daily routine can yield a plethora of advantages. These benefits include increased self-esteem, improved focus, reduced stress and anxiety, and enhanced overall well-being. By consistently speaking affirmations to oneself, individuals can reprogram their subconscious mind, replacing negative self-talk with positive and empowering statements. As a result, they can cultivate a more positive outlook on life and achieve their goals with greater confidence and ease.

If you struggle with negative thoughts and beliefs about yourself, incorporating affirmations into your daily routine can be a powerful way to boost your self-esteem. When repeated regularly, these uplifting statements can help reframe your mindset and replace negative self-talk with positive affirmations. Focusing on your strengths and abilities can cultivate a more confident and self-assured outlook on life.

Whether you write your claims or seek out pre-made ones online, incorporating these positive messages into your daily life can profoundly impact your overall well-being.

Affirming oneself has been proven to be highly effective in increasing motivation and maintaining a strong focus on one's goals. By regularly utilizing this practice, individuals can reinforce positive thoughts and beliefs, ultimately leading to a more confident and booming mindset. Whether through verbal or written affirmations, the power of self-affirmation should be considered.

One effective way to alleviate stress is by practicing affirmations. Doing so gives you the power to transform negative thoughts and beliefs you may hold about the world. This can help you cultivate a more positive and optimistic outlook on life, ultimately benefiting your overall well-being. So, why not try affirmations and see how they work wonders for your mental health?

If you struggle with negative thoughts and beliefs about others, incorporating affirmations into your daily routine can be immensely beneficial in improving your relationships. You can cultivate a healthier and more fulfilling connection with those around you by consistently practicing positive self-talk and shifting your mindset toward a more optimistic outlook. So why not try it and see its positive impact on your life?

To achieve your deepest desires, it's essential to understand the power of affirmations. By consistently repeating positive statements to yourself, you can effectively alter your subconscious beliefs, affirming that your desires have already been confirmed. This technique can help you manifest your goals and live your desired life.

How to use affirmations:

There are numerous techniques to make the most of affirmations. If you want to enhance your personal growth and well-being, here are a few suggestions. First and foremost, choosing affirmations that resonate with you profoundly is essential. These should be statements that inspire and motivate you and that feel authentic to your values and aspirations. Once you've identified your affirmations, repeating them regularly throughout the day can be helpful, either aloud or silently.

Consider writing them down or creating visual reminders to keep them top of mind. Finally, be patient and persistent in your affirmation practice; it may take time to see results, but with consistent effort, you can cultivate a more positive and empowered mindset.

Many people find it helpful to use affirmations to boost their confidence and improve their mindset. One popular method is to repeat affirmations in front of a mirror or by recording oneself and listening to the recording multiple times. This process can effectively affirm positive beliefs about oneself and promote a positive outlook. By regularly practicing affirmations, individuals can cultivate a more optimistic and self-assured mindset to help them achieve their goals and live more fulfilling lives.

Experts suggest posting affirmations in a physical journal or on paper to cultivate a positive mindset. Consistently reviewing these affirmations can reinforce their message and impact on your daily life. A helpful tip is to consider placing these affirmations in locations where you frequently spend time, such as on your bathroom mirror or refrigerator, as a reminder of their importance.

One effective technique to help you reach your goals is visualization. Take a few moments to close your eyes and imagine yourself accomplishing everything you desire. Picture yourself as successful, confident, and filled with joy. By visualizing your desired outcome, you can help bring it into reality.

Dedicating much of your day to practicing meditation and focusing on your affirmations is highly recommended. Doing so allows your claims of powerful and positive messages to penetrate deep into your consciousness and become a part of your very being. Such a practice can tremendously benefit your overall well-being and help you cultivate a more positive and purposeful mindset. So, take the time to prioritize this practice and see the incredible effects it can have on your life.

Affirmations are a powerful tool that can help you to improve your life in many ways.

Affirmations are a great place to start if you want to change your thoughts and beliefs, improve your self-esteem, or achieve your goals.

Here are some additional tips for using affirmations:

When reprogramming your subconscious mind, exercising patience and understanding is crucial. This is because the process can take quite some time, requiring repetition to start seeing the desired results. It's important to note that you shouldn't expect immediate changes as it can be discouraging if you don't see any significant difference immediately.

Instead, trust in the process and give it some time to work. With dedication and persistence, you can successfully reprogram your subconscious mind to achieve your goals and aspirations.

Maintaining consistency is crucial when it comes to affirmations. It is important to repeat them frequently to achieve their maximum effectiveness. The more regularly you repeat your claims, the more they will become ingrained in your subconscious mind, leading to positive changes in your thoughts, emotions, and behavior. Therefore, it is recommended to make affirmations a regular part of your daily routine to achieve the desired results.

Believing in oneself and having faith in the truth of affirmations is crucial to achieving success and personal growth. The subconscious mind can only accept claims believed to be accurate, so it's essential to cultivate a strong sense of self-belief to ensure the effectiveness of positive affirmations. By trusting in oneself and the power of affirmations, individuals can tap into the potential of their minds and achieve their desired outcomes.

Do you have the desire to create the life you've always wanted? If so, are you willing to dedicate the time and energy needed to make it happen? Utilizing affirmations can be an incredibly effective method for achieving your desired outcomes. Don't hesitate any longer; immediately incorporate affirmations into your daily routine!

How to do affirmations in accessing bliss?

Attaining a profound sense of joy and satisfaction that brings about a feeling of tranquility with ourselves and our surroundings is what experiencing bliss is all about. It can be achieved through various methods but one of the most effective ways to access this state is by practicing affirmations—positive statements that reinforce our beliefs and values and help us cultivate a positive mindset.

By repeating affirmations regularly, we can train our minds to focus on the good things in life and, ultimately, experience a sense of bliss that permeates every aspect of our existence.

Repeating positive affirmations can effectively reprogram our subconscious mind to adopt new and empowering beliefs. This transformation process occurs gradually as our repeated assertions shift our thoughts, emotions, and, ultimately, our actions. As we persist in this practice, we can cultivate a more joyful and satisfying life experience, gradually moving closer to complete happiness. Committing to positive affirmation can shape our inner reality and create a life filled with abundance, joy, and fulfillment.

Here are some tips for using affirmations to access bliss:

When choosing affirmations, keeping a few key factors in mind is essential. Firstly, specificity is critical—the more detailed and tailored your claim is to your unique situation, the more effective it will be. Secondly, it's essential to focus on positive language—rather than framing your affirmation in terms of what you want to avoid or eliminate from your life, try to focus on what you want to invite in and cultivate.

Finally, phrasing your affirmation in the present tense can help you fully embody the feeling or attitude you're trying to develop. For example, instead of saying, "I will be happy", try framing it as "I am currently feeling happy and content". This can help you tap into the power of the present moment and feel more connected to your affirmation on a deeper level.

Developing a practice of regularly repeating your positive affirmations can significantly impact your subconscious mind. Consistency is critical as the more you repeat these affirmations, the more profoundly they will take root and influence your thoughts and actions. By making this a habit, you empower yourself to cultivate a more positive and productive mindset. Remember, positive thinking is accurate, and by incorporating daily affirmations into your routine, you can harness this power to improve your overall well-being.

When you practice reciting your affirmations, allow yourself a few moments to envision yourself triumphantly reaching your desired outcomes. This technique will foster a sense of belief within you, empowering you to see your goals as already attainable.

Meditation might be the answer if you're looking for a powerful way to truly absorb and integrate your affirmations. By taking regular time to sit in stillness and focus your mind, you can create a space to concentrate on your positive declarations. This means that you can let the uplifting messages you're telling yourself sink in and become a part of your subconscious. Over time, this can lead to a decisive shift in your mindset and a more profound sense of inner peace and positivity. So why try it and see how it can transform your life?

Please exercise patience and keep in mind that altering your subconscious mind may require a considerable amount of time and effort. It's essential to understand that the outcome may not be instantaneous but if you persist and stay dedicated, you will eventually see positive results.

Having faith in oneself and recognizing one's worthiness of joy and contentment is crucial. It's important to understand that our subconscious mind tends to mimic the beliefs we hold about ourselves. Therefore, if we believe that we deserve happiness and fulfillment, our subconscious mind will follow suit and work toward achieving that state.

Here are some examples of affirmations that you can use to access bliss:

- I am happy and content.
- I am surrounded by love and abundance.
- I am grateful for all that I have.
- I am at peace with myself and with the world.
- I am living my best life.

Greetings! It is my pleasure to offer you some examples of affirmations that may be of assistance to you. However, please modify them to suit your distinct requirements and goals. What is crucial is to select affirmations that resonate with you and bring positivity to your mindset.

If you consistently incorporate affirmations into your daily routine, you'll eventually see positive changes in your life. These changes can include an increased sense of happiness, contentment, and inner peace, which can help you to achieve your goals and live a more fulfilling life overall. So don't hesitate to practice affirmations today and experience the joy and fulfillment you truly deserve!

Here are some additional tips for using affirmations to access bliss:

For optimal results, it is advisable to seek a serene location devoid of disruptions or disturbances that impede one's focus and productivity.

If you find yourself feeling anxious or distracted, it can be helpful to take a moment to focus on your breath. Try taking a few slow, deep breaths, inhaling through your nose, and exhaling through your mouth. Try to focus on the sensation of the breath moving in and out of your body as you breathe. This simple technique can help calm your mind and bring you back to the present moment.

One effective way to reinforce your positive affirmations is to repeat them regularly. This can be achieved by vocalizing them audibly or silently reciting them. By doing this consistently, you can cultivate a habit of positive thinking and enhance your overall well-being.

Picture yourself achieving all the goals you have set for yourself with ease and confidence. Envision the satisfaction and pride of accomplishing what you set out to do. See yourself basking in the glory of success, knowing that your hard work and dedication have paid off. Allow yourself to revel in the joy of your achievements, knowing you have what it takes to make your dreams a reality.

Indulge in the gratifying sensations of successfully achieving your desired goals and objectives. The feeling of accomplishment and fulfillment is genuinely uplifting and can boost your confidence and motivation to pursue even more significant achievements in the future.

Before concluding your session, it would be beneficial to pause and reflect on the abundance of blessings in your life. Take a moment to acknowledge and appreciate all you have as it will promote a sense of gratitude and contentment.

It is highly recommended that you repeat your affirmations daily to achieve the best results. However, increasing the frequency of your commitments is advisable if you are facing overwhelming stress or anxiety. By practicing consistently, you will start noticing positive changes in your life. You will experience greater happiness, contentment, and inner peace.

Moreover, you will be more likely to accomplish your objectives and live a satisfying life. So, make sure to prioritize the repetition of your affirmations to reap the benefits that come with it.

There's no need to put off the benefits of affirmations any longer. By incorporating positive affirmations into your daily routine, you can experience the joy and happiness you deserve. So why not start today? With consistent practice, you'll see the positive impact that affirmations can have on your life.

What are the benefits of affirmations in accessing bliss?

Bliss is a desirable state of being that embodies a sense of unbridled pleasure and contentment. It involves feeling entirely comfortable in one's skin and the world around them. Utilizing affirmations is an incredibly efficacious technique to attain this state of bliss. By employing such positive statements, individuals can take ownership of their happiness and cultivate a sense of inner peace that knows no bounds.

Through repetition, we can reprogram our subconscious mind with positive affirmations, which in turn can transform our beliefs, thoughts, emotions, and actions. As we continue to nurture and reinforce these new beliefs, we can experience a profound shift in our overall outlook and approach to life.

By embracing this process, we open ourselves up to a more fulfilling and joyful existence, ultimately reaching a state of bliss that is both empowering and life-affirming.

There are numerous benefits to utilizing affirmations to attain a state of bliss. These positive statements can assist in fostering a more optimistic outlook, increasing self-confidence, and enhancing overall well-being. Claims can also be a powerful tool for overcoming negative self-talk and limiting beliefs, allowing individuals to manifest their desired outcomes and achieve their goals. By regularly incorporating affirmations into one's daily routine, it is possible to cultivate a more positive and fulfilling life experience.

It has been shown that consistently repeating positive affirmations can significantly impact our self-esteem. By intentionally replacing negative thoughts and beliefs with affirmations that reinforce our worthiness of love, happiness, and success, we can experience a positive shift in our overall mindset and confidence in our capabilities. This simple yet powerful practice can help us to cultivate a more positive self-image and ultimately lead to a more fulfilling life.

Positive affirmations can be transformative for managing stress and improving our overall well-being. By actively working to change or challenge our negative thoughts and beliefs, we can cultivate a more positive outlook on life and greater control over our experiences.

When we regularly repeat positive affirmations to ourselves, we begin to internalize these messages and genuinely believe in our ability to overcome obstacles and navigate life's challenges with ease and grace. This can help reduce anxiety or overwhelm and promote a greater sense of calm and peace in our daily lives.

Positive affirmations can transform our mindset and promote a more positive outlook on life. By embracing optimistic and encouraging claims, we can reshape our negative thoughts and beliefs about joy, ultimately reinforcing the idea that we are deserving of happiness and capable of manifesting it in our lives. This shift in perspective can significantly impact our overall well-being, leading to increased levels of contentment and fulfillment in our daily experiences.

The act of affirming oneself and others has the potential to significantly improve our relationships. By replacing negative thoughts and beliefs with positive affirmations, we reinforce the idea that everyone deserves love and respect. This mindset helps us become more open and accepting toward others, strengthening our relationships and making them more fulfilling. Through the power of affirmations, we can create a more positive and harmonious environment for ourselves and those around us.

If we possess a profound yearning to accomplish something, practicing affirmations is exceedingly advantageous in aiding us to achieve our objectives. By consistently repeating affirmative statements about our desires, we can alter our subconscious minds to believe that our aspirations are already validated. This can instill a sense of assurance and inspiration to take decisive steps toward our passions, thus enabling us to eventually realize our goals.

Incorporating affirmations into our daily routine can significantly improve our overall well-being and success. Whether we desire to shift our mindset and perspectives, strengthen our self-assurance, or achieve our goals and aspirations, affirmations are a valuable tool for initiating positive change. By consistently repeating uplifting statements tailored to our specific needs and desires, we can cultivate a more optimistic outlook and attract abundance into our lives.

Thank you for your interest in learning more about using affirmations to reach a state of bliss. Allow me to provide additional suggestions to help you achieve this goal. Firstly, it's essential to be specific and intentional with your affirmations. Instead of saying, "I am happy", try saying, "I am radiating joy and positivity in all aspects of my life". This will help you focus on the feeling you want to cultivate and attract more of it into your life.

Additionally, try incorporating affirmations into your daily routine, such as saying them while brushing your teeth or during your morning meditation. Finally, remember to honestly believe in the power of your affirmations and trust that the universe will bring you what you desire. With these tips in mind, you'll be well on your way to experiencing a state of bliss and inner peace.

It is essential to remember that reprogramming your subconscious mind is a gradual process that requires patience and consistency. While you may not see immediate results, staying committed to the process and trusting that progress will come with time is essential. Remember to be kind and patient with yourself throughout this journey. You will see positive changes in your mindset and behavior with persistence and repetition.

If you want to maximize the effectiveness of your affirmations, it's crucial to maintain a consistent practice of repeating them regularly. This repetition helps to embed the claims more deeply in your subconscious mind, making them more impactful and enduring. Committing to a daily routine of reciting your affirmations can cultivate a more positive and empowering mindset over time. So, prioritize the repetition of your claims and watch as they transform your life for the better.

Believing in oneself is a significant aspect of affirmations. It is essential to have complete confidence in the validity of your claims to allow your subconscious mind to accept them. Trust in your declarations is necessary to materialize their positive impact on your life. Therefore, it is vital to trust in yourself and the power of your affirmations to experience their full benefits.

If you're willing to invest the required time and energy, incorporating affirmations into your daily routine can be a powerful tool in manifesting the life you've always dreamed of. Don't delay any further; start practicing positive affirmations today and unlock the joy and fulfillment you deserve.

Chapter 9: Conclusion

How to maintain a state of bliss in your life

Attaining a state of complete happiness and contentment is what we refer to as experiencing bliss. This state is characterized by inner peace and harmony with our surroundings. While it may seem challenging to maintain such a state, various practical tools and practices can help us achieve it. By incorporating these tools and techniques into our daily lives, we can cultivate a sense of bliss that can positively impact our overall well-being.

It brings me great joy to offer practical advice on sustaining happiness within oneself.

If you're looking to improve your overall well-being, there are several simple yet effective tips that you can incorporate into your daily routine. Practicing mindfulness is one of the most powerful ways to cultivate greater inner peace. Mindfulness involves being fully present at the moment without judgment, allowing you to appreciate the good things in your life and let go of negative thoughts and emotions that can hold you back from feeling truly happy.

Incorporating meditation into your daily routine is another great way to boost your well-being. With so many different types of meditation available, there is sure to be one that resonates with you. Whether you prefer guided meditations, silent meditations, or something in between, regular practice can help you train your mind to focus on the present moment and let go of distractions that might be causing you stress or anxiety.

In addition to mindfulness and meditation, spending time in nature can profoundly impact your well-being. Whether you enjoy hiking, biking, or simply taking a leisurely stroll through a local park or nature reserve, being surrounded by the beauty of the natural world can help you feel more relaxed, calm, and at peace.

Another way to improve your happiness and well-being is to make time for activities you love. This might include reading, spending time with loved ones, pursuing a hobby, or engaging in any other activity that brings you joy and fulfillment. You can create a more meaningful and satisfying life by prioritizing the things that matter most to you.

Incorporating the habits of gratitude and forgiveness into your daily routine can significantly impact your overall well-being. By setting aside a few moments each day to reflect on the various aspects of your life that you are grateful for, you can establish a more profound appreciation for the good things around you. This newfound gratitude can translate into greater happiness, contentment, and fulfillment, ultimately leading to a more fulfilling life experience. Additionally, practicing forgiveness can help relieve resentment and negativity, allowing you to move forward with a more positive outlook. By embracing these healthy habits, you can cultivate a more balanced and fulfilled existence, ultimately leading to a higher quality of life overall.

Maintaining a consistent sense of happiness and contentment is a goal many strive for, but it can only be challenging with the proper tools and practices. Fortunately, several tips and strategies can help you achieve a life full of joy and tranquility. In addition to the suggestions above, there are several other ways to maintain a state of bliss.

By incorporating practices such as mindfulness meditation, regular exercise, and spending time in nature, you can cultivate a sense of inner peace and happiness that will sustain you throughout your daily life. Additionally, making time for self-care activities, such as relaxing or reading a good book, can help you unwind and recharge, allowing you to approach each day with renewed energy and positivity.

With dedication and commitment, anyone can achieve a state of happiness and contentment that will enrich their life and bring them lasting joy.

It is crucial to avoid individuals and influences that emit negativity, as they can drain our energy and impede our ability to feel content. If you discover yourself in an environment with pessimism, you may need to alter your surroundings and lifestyle to cultivate a more positive atmosphere.

Taking care of oneself is crucial to leading a healthy and fulfilling life. This involves paying attention to our physical well-being by eating nutritious foods, getting adequate rest, and exercising regularly. When we prioritize these habits, we can experience positive effects on our physical health and emotional and mental states. Therefore, it is essential to make self-care a top priority in our daily routine.

It is imperative to establish appropriate boundaries to prevent ourselves from taking on too much. When we give too much of ourselves to others, it can result in feelings of being overwhelmed, drained, and stressed out. Therefore, it is essential to set clear limits and communicate them effectively to maintain our emotional and physical well-being. By doing so, we can protect ourselves from feeling burned out and ensure that we can show up as our best selves in all our lives.

Trusting our gut feeling is an essential aspect of decision-making. Our intuition is a valuable tool that guides us toward choices that align with our best interests. When we pay close attention to our intuition, we increase our likelihood of staying on track and avoiding options that could lead us astray from happiness. Therefore, listening to our inner voice and trusting our instincts to make the right decisions is crucial.

You can realize profound inner joy and fulfillment with unwavering dedication and a commitment to investing time and effort into your personal growth. The key to achieving this state of being is to follow the guidance and recommendations outlined above. By doing so, you can create a genuinely fulfilling life in which happiness, peace, and contentment are ever-present. So, take the necessary steps to cultivate inner bliss and allow yourself to bask in the many benefits of living in profound joy and happiness.

Thank You

Dear Readers,

A heartfelt thank you for embarking on this journey of self-discovery through "Bliss: Access Within You." I hope the words and insights shared within these pages have resonated with you, sparking a deeper connection to your inner joy and peace.

May this book's practices guide your path, illuminating the boundless potential for bliss within you. Remember, the journey to inner peace is ongoing, and I sincerely wish that you continue to nurture and cultivate the seeds of joy that have been planted.

With gratitude and warmest wishes,
Dr. Shanthi Ramaiah